FRESH THAI

OI CHEEPCHAIISSARA

hamlyn

**TO MY PARENTS WHO PROVIDED
ALL THE GOOD THINGS IN LIFE,
INCLUDING WONDERFUL FOOD
FOR OUR FAMILY**

First published in Great Britain in 2007 by
Hamlyn, a division of Octopus Publishing Group Ltd
2–4 Heron Quays, London E14 4JP

Copyright © Octopus Publishing Group Ltd 2007

The material in this book was previously published
in *Fresh Thai*

ISBN-13: 978-0-600-61685-6
ISBN-10: 0-600-61685-1

A CIP catalogue record for this book is available
from the British Library

Printed and bound in China

10 9 8 7 6 5 4 3 2 1

NOTE

Both metric and imperial measurements have been given
in all recipes. Use one set of measurements only, and not
a mixture of both.

Standard level spoon measurements are used in all recipes.
1 tablespoon = one 15 ml spoon
1 teaspoon = one 5 ml spoon

The Department of Health advises that eggs should not be
consumed raw. This book contains dishes made with raw or
lightly cooked eggs. It is prudent for vulnerable people such as
pregnant and nursing mothers, invalids, the elderly, babies and
young children to avoid uncooked or lightly cooked dishes
made with eggs. Once prepared, these dishes should be kept
refrigerated and used promptly.

This book includes dishes made with nuts and nut derivatives.
It is advisable for those with known allergic reactions to nuts
and nut derivatives and those who may be potentially
vulnerable to these allergies, such as pregnant and nursing
mothers, invalids, the elderly, babies and children to avoid
dishes made with nuts and nut oils. It is also prudent to check
the labels of pre-prepared ingredients for the possible inclusion
of nut derivatives.

Ovens should be preheated to the specified temperature
– if using a fan-assisted oven, follow the manufacturer's
instructions for adjusting the time and the temperature.

CONTENTS

INTRODUCTION

In Thailand we are passionate about our food. When my family gets together my aunts and cousins usually bring their favourite dishes to add to an already sumptuous spread. This often results in a surfeit of food – but nobody minds. We eat it gradually throughout the day, knowing that there will be no adverse effects.

Our tendency to indulge in good food without putting on weight has attracted the attention of visitors from other countries. How do we do it, they wonder? There is no simple answer. Our intensely hot climate sometimes makes us sweat and expel excess salt, yet air-conditioning is widely used. We enjoy sports, but I doubt if we exercise more than anyone else. So it must be the food. It is surely the freshness of Thai food – our love of fruit and vegetables straight from the market, seafood straight from the sea and, above all, fresh herbs rather than powdered spices – that makes our cuisine beneficial to everyone who eats it.

COOKING IN THE THAI STYLE

Learning to cook Thai, if you are not yourself Thai, is perfectly feasible – and great fun. Our cuisine is not vast, but it is certainly varied, with influences from China, India and the Muslim countries to the south. If you think Thai you will soon find yourself thinking about coconut, ginger, lemon grass, garlic, galangal, coriander, fish sauce, hot chillies and jasmine rice.

The Thai style of cooking is different from the Western approach. In this book I bridge the gap by providing tested measurements that will enable you to obtain excellent results if you follow the directions precisely. However, Thai cooks tend to rely on tasting rather than measurement. From long experience they can tell exactly when a dish has that unique combination of ingredients that makes it authentic. To reach this level of expertise you will need to get into the spirit of Thai cooking, and with this in mind I offer the following advice.

Try to achieve a balanced taste, both in individual dishes and in the meal as a whole. Underlying Thai cuisine are the five flavours: sweet, sour, salty, bitter and hot. We derive sweetness from palm sugar, cane sugar and from sweet fruit such as pineapples; sourness comes from lime, lemon and vinegar; saltiness from fish sauce and shrimp paste; bitter melon provides the bitter taste that is occasionally introduced into the larger meals; and heat comes from both fresh and dried chillies. Combine these flavours in a harmonious way – not necessarily in equal proportions – and you are beginning to cook in the Thai spirit.

Presentation is an integral part of Thai cooking, and the food must appeal to the eye as well as the palate. Here we are dealing with colours, shapes and textures, using garnishes such as finely sliced red chillies to contrast with the green of the coriander or the whiteness of the rice. There is no need to prepare elaborate fruit and vegetable carvings, which adorn the tables at weddings and other feasts, but it is easy to learn how to make a few deft cuts in a long chilli and watch it splay out into a beautiful flower shape when you place it in a bowl of water. With a few touches like this your home-prepared meal will look as well as taste authentically Thai.

ACHIEVING AUTHENTICITY

In the cooking classes that I have run for several years I always introduce people to dishes that really are authentic, just like those you can eat in Thailand. I am not entirely against adaptation, however. It is sometimes necessary because finding authentic ingredients for a particular dish may be difficult. It can be quite acceptable – even preferable – to substitute a locally grown, fresh vegetable for an imported Thai one and still retain an authentic Thai flavour from the herbs and sauces.

There is no need to be too rigid in attempting to use fresh herbs and vegetables on every occasion. For example, dried chillies are an essential ingredient in Thai cooking, and they impart a stronger flavour and aroma than fresh chillies. It is worth remembering that some frozen vegetables (peas are a good example) can actually be more nutritious than their market-fresh equivalents. You will still get acceptable results if you buy plenty of lemon grass, ginger and other vital ingredients and store them in the freezer. You can also keep the labour-intensive curry pastes in the freezer for several weeks, using them as they are needed.

COOKING FOR HEALTH

For this book I have made some minor adaptations to my traditional recipes in order to enhance their health benefits. You will notice that there are no deep-fried dishes. I have also reduced the amount of salt while making sure that the food still tastes delicious. In many of the stir-fry dishes I have used sunflower oil, which is popular in Thailand. I use a nonstick wok rather than an iron wok, and I urge you to do the same. In this way you can cook successfully with just a tiny amount of oil, keeping all the fats to a minimum.

In Thailand there is a large industry that processes coconuts to make coconut cream and coconut milk. In rich food coconut cream is delicious, but here I have kept a good flavour by using a half-measure of coconut milk with its lower fat content, together with a half-measure of either stock or water. The result, I hope you will agree, is very acceptable – and with luck it will help you to live longer to enjoy more good food.

REGIONAL VARIATIONS

The recipes in this book are based on dishes from all the regions of Thailand, but mostly from the central plain, which is dominated by Bangkok, and the southern peninsula. This is because I was born in the south, in Hat Yai, but went to college in Bangkok where I later worked. I have travelled to the other regions, frequently to the mountainous north but also to the dry land to the east. Each region has a distinctive cuisine, but they all tend to get mixed up in the vast metropolis of Bangkok.

In the north, people enjoy milder curries, glutinous (sticky) rice and specialities like spicy pork sausages. From the central plain come favourite dishes such as hot and sour soup, green curry, and chicken, coconut and galangal soup. In the south we love hot curries – and the seafood is exceptional.

SERVING THAI FOOD

If you are going to cook Thai food at home it will be most effective if you follow Thai custom and serve all the dishes at the same time. Visitors are often surprised by this practice, expecting to start with a separate soup course, followed by fish and meat dishes.

But having everything together, except dessert, is the only way to enjoy Thai food properly. You need to be able to dilute the powerful flavours of the soups with a spoonful of rice or share the special fish dishes among your guests.

To help you create some balanced Thai meals I have made some menu suggestions, but please add your favourite dishes if I have not included them. It is essential to have steamed rice and customary to have soup, a curry dish or a spicy salad, a vegetable dish and a dipping sauce. In the south we nearly always have fish or seafood as an option, while dishes based on tofu are becoming increasingly popular.

Although we eat plenty of fish and seafood and relatively little red meat, many Thais are strict vegetarians. In their home cooking they substitute the usual fish sauce with soy sauce, or shrimp paste with soya bean paste. It can require more imagination to make vegetarian dishes truly tasty, but Thai chilli sauces and relishes are great in salads or mixed into stir-fries with tofu.

With so many starters, soups and main dishes it may be surprising to find that we are fond of desserts, some of which are delightfully cooling. What could be better on a hot summer day than Watermelon Sorbet? Or, if the weather is colder, try Black Sticky Rice with Egg Custard, if you are not already *im* (full).

There are many traditions in Thai cooking but no fixed rules. Centuries ago we tried the chillies brought to us by the Portuguese; now it is hard to imagine Thai cooking without them. Our cuisine is constantly evolving and we love to try new tastes to see if they will harmonize. Now it is your turn to cook something fresh. It is time to start cooking Fresh Thai.

PREPARING SEAFOOD

Careful preparation will greatly improve your seafood dishes. In Thailand food is quick to cook but takes time to prepare.

CRAB To remove the cool cooked crab meat from the shell, lay the crab on its back and twist off the legs and claws. Cover it with polythene or a cloth and crack the legs and claws by tapping them with a rolling pin or a small hammer. Use a skewer or pick to remove the flesh. Discard the cartilage and membranes. Place the crab on its back, push up the apron with your thumbs and sepa-

rate it from the shell. Remove and discard the spongy gills, as the lungs are sometimes called. Use a skewer to pick out the white meat and place it in a bowl. Press down on the mouth of the shell to crack it away. Discard the cartilage, membrane and stomach sac, all of which are found in the shell. Remove the soft brown meat. Crack the under-shell and remove it at the joint. Clean out the shell and use the white and dark meat, or shell, as required. Alternatively, ask your fishmonger to cook and shell crabs for you.

Live, uncooked crabs should be scrubbed and put in the freezer for 30 minutes to firm up the flesh. Twist off and remove the upper shell and discard the stomach sac and the soft gill tissue. Leaving the legs attached, cut the crab in half through the centre of the shell from head to rear. Then cut it in half again from left to right, quartering the crab and leaving the legs attached to each quarter. Using a cracker or the back of a heavy knife, crack the crab claws to make them easier to eat.

FISH Whole flat fish, such as plaice, turbot, snapper, sea bream and sea bass, should be cleaned and gutted but the head left on. Score with a sharp knife three or four times on both sides and dry thoroughly.

To prepare whole round fish, such as trout, mackerel and red or grey mullet, hold the fish firmly by tail and, if necessary, scrape with a knife from tail to head to remove the excess scales. Trim the fins and cut the tail into a neat V with scissors. Lay the fish on a chopping board. With a sharp knife slit the belly; scrape and discard the gut. Leave the head on if you wish. Clean and score with a sharp knife, making three or four slashes in each side. You can ask your fishmonger to prepare the fish for you if you are short of time.

MUSSELS AND CLAMS Clean and scrub mussels or clams with a stiff brush. Throw away any empty shells and any that are cracked or open. Use a small, sharp knife to scrape away the beard from the mussels. Wash both mussels and clams in several changes of cold

water until the water is left clean. Put them in a large bowl, cover with cold water and leave to stand for 30 minutes. Drain and set aside.

PRAWNS Use fresh, medium to large prawns. Clean and pinch off the legs and head, then peel and devein the prawns to remove the intestinal tract (the black line). Cut them open like a butterfly but leave the halves joined at the tails. You do not need to devein small prawns.

SCALLOPS All my scallop recipes use both types of meat found in the shell: the white, meaty part and the coral which is the bright orange roe. To prepare, grip the scallop in one hand using a tea towel, insert a knife or special tool and twist open the shell. Remove the meat with a knife and trim off the dark strings of intestinal tract.

SQUID Pull the body away from the head and tentacles. Open the tentacles, then press the hard part of the head so that the 'beak' comes out. Discard it. Cut off the tentacles. Empty the squid pouches and pull off the purplish skin. Rinse the squid and tentacles thoroughly. Use the body for stuffing, cut it into rings or cut it in half and open the body pouches. Lightly score the outside of each squid with a sharp knife, making diagonal cross cuts to form a diamond pattern and cut into pieces about 4 cm (1½ inches) square.

STORECUPBOARD INGREDIENTS

Many of the ingredients used in the recipes in this book are available in large supermarkets, but some of them will be found only in oriental or specialist Thai shops. If there are no specialist retailers in your area you can also purchase these ingredients on the Internet.

BEAN SAUCE Black bean sauce is made from fermented black beans and is used to add a salty taste to stir-fried meat, vegetables or seafood. Yellow bean sauce, which also imparts saltiness, is made from yellow soya beans and is often added to chicken, pork or vegetable stir-fries.

COCONUT MILK A low-fat version of coconut milk with 65 per cent less fat than regular coconut milk is available, but my method of using a half measure of regular coconut milk and water or stock will give similar results.

CORIANDER ROOT The root of the coriander is used only in Thai cuisine, so its inclusion in a recipe makes a dish particularly authentic. The leaves are used as a gar-

nish, but the roots are used in pastes and in any dish that needs the full flavour of coriander. It can be found in Thai and oriental supermarkets.

DRIED BLACK FUNGUS A popular ingredient in stir-fries and vegetarian dishes, dried black fungus, or cloud ears, are thin, ruffle-edged, black mushrooms. They are similar in appearance to wood ears but are slightly smaller, lighter in colour and have a more delicate flavour. Use them to add a crunchy texture to a dish. Soften them in hot water for a few minutes before using them.

GROUND DRIED SHRIMP Known as *kung haeng*, this is the result of grinding dried shrimp until they become fluffy. It is widely used in traditional Thai cooking.

GROUND RICE This dry-fry rice is made by frying jasmine rice in a pan over medium heat. Put 2 tablespoons of jasmine rice in a small pan and fry for 6–8 minutes or until brown, shaking the pan continually to move the rice around the pan. Use a pestle and mortar or a small blender to grind the rice to a powder. Keep it in an airtight jar and use it as required.

KAFFIR LIME LEAVES These are among the most important ingredients in Thai cuisine and give their best flavour when they are fresh rather than dry or frozen. They are readily available in most large supermarkets.

LEMON GRASS This is available in most supermarkets these days. The wonderful, lemony flavour comes from the white part, near the base of the stem.

LESSER GINGER Smaller and with a more intense flavour than ginger, fresh lesser ginger (*krachai*) can be bought in Thai and oriental supermarkets. It should be thinly peeled and finely sliced before use.

NOODLES Noodles come in many different shapes and sizes, and can be either fresh or dry. Fresh noodles can be found in the refrigerated section of your oriental market. Dry noodles also come in bundles kept in plastic bags. Rice noodles are made from a paste of rice flour and water, which is steamed in large trays and then cut into different widths. *Sen yai* or wide noodles are about 2 cm (I inch) wide; *sen lek* are less than 5 mm (¼ inch) wide; and *sen mii* vermicelli are very thin indeed, just over 1 mm (¹⁄₁₆ inch) thick. Rice flake noodles

(*kuay chap*) are big, flat noodles the size of tortilla chips. There are also non-rice noodles, such as wheat noodles (*ba mii*), which are made with egg; and mung bean starch noodles (*wun sen*), which, like *sen mii*, are sometimes called vermicelli. Most of the dry noodles need to be soaked in water at room temperature for 4–5 hours or overnight; this prevents them breaking up when they are cooked.

OIL Sunflower oil is high in polyunsaturates, which are believed to break down cholesterol. Sesame oil, which is made from roasted sesame seeds, can be used sparingly for its aroma and rich flavour.

PALM OR COCONUT SUGAR These sugars, available in jars or cake form, are used in Thai cooking because they are local products. If you cannot find them use brown (demerara) sugar instead.

PAPAYAS These fruits turn from green to yellow-orange as they ripen. In supermarkets they are often sold partially ripe, but you need to hunt for a green one in a Thai or Asian supermarket for the classic dish of green papaya salad.

THAI JASMINE RICE Rice is essential in Thai cooking and is served at all meals. The best variety to use for Thai cuisine is jasmine rice with its natural, delicate fragrance. Brown rice has plenty of vitamins and comes in smaller bags than jasmine rice. Bags of rice can be kept in the storecupboard for at least a year. White and black sticky rice are used for desserts but accompaniments to some of the Thai dishes can also have a sticky texture.

POMELO The pomelo is related to the grapefruit, which can be used as an alternative, but its skin is much thicker than that of an orange or grapefruit. To peel it, slice a circular patch off the top of the fruit, about 5 mm (¼ inch) deep (roughly the thickness of the skin). Then score six deep lines from top to bottom, dividing the skin into five segments. Now peel off the skin, one segment at a time. Remove any remaining pith and separate the segments of the fruit. Crumble the segments into their component parts, without squashing them or releasing the juice.

THAI SWEET BASIL Often used for garnishing, Thai sweet basil *bai horapha* has purple stems and a unique taste and fragrance. Although you can use other types of basil with acceptable results, the dishes will not be completely authentic.

PRESERVED RADISH Known as *chai poh*, preserved radish is crunchy and spicy and has a touch of sweetness and saltiness. It is finely chopped and sold in vacuum packs and jars in Thai and oriental supermarkets.

TOFU Available in soft, silky and firm forms, tofu or beancurd can be bought fresh or in long-life packs. Soft tofu can be served with fresh herbs and dressing, in soup dishes and for dessert. Firm tofu is used for stir-fries and is added to curry dishes.

SHREDDED COCONUT This is a useful ingredient to keep in the storecupboard. It can be spread on salads. Sweetened or unsweetened, it is available in packets from Thai and oriental supermarkets. If you want to remove the sugar from sweetened coconut, soak it in a mixture of half-milk, half-water for an hour in the refrigerator. Drain it and pat dry, and it is ready for use.

WRAPPERS Spring roll sheets, filo pastry sheets (thawed before use) and fresh won ton sheets can be kept in the refrigerator for a few days. All of these wrappers can be kept in the freezer for at least 3 months.

MENU PLANS

MENU FOR 2 PEOPLE

Garlic prawns

Red curry chicken with Thai baby
  aubergines (½ quantity)

Boiled jasmine rice

Quail eggs in ginger syrup
  (½ quantity)

MENU FOR 2 PEOPLE

Stir-fried mushrooms with ginger

Green curry beef with bamboo
  shoots

Boiled jasmine rice

Watermelon sorbet

MENU FOR 2 PEOPLE

Spring-flowering chives with squid

Panaeng chicken curry (½ quantity)

Boiled jasmine rice

Sticky rice with mango (½ quantity)

FAMILY MENU FOR 4 PEOPLE

Barbecued pork spare ribs

Steamed fish with chilli and lime juice

Green curry beef with bamboo
  shoots

Stir-fried mushrooms with ginger

Boiled jasmine rice

Sticky rice with mango

FAMILY MENU FOR 4 PEOPLE

Grilled seafood with pineapple

Stir-fried mixed vegetables

Panaeng chicken curry

Hot and sour seafood soup

Boiled jasmine rice

Sago pudding with white
  lotus seeds

FAMILY SEAFOOD MENU FOR 4 PEOPLE

Fishcakes with green beans
  served with cucumber relish

Black sesame seeds with prawns
  and water chestnuts

Red curry with fish and tofu

Stir-fried mixed vegetables

Boiled jasmine rice

Quail eggs in ginger syrup

FAMILY MENU FOR 6 PEOPLE

Golden baskets

Sweet and sour mixed
  vegetables

Garlic prawns

Red curry chicken with Thai
  baby aubergines

Bean sprouts and tofu soup

Boiled jasmine rice

Black sticky rice with egg custard
  (make double quantities)

FAMILY MENU FOR 6 PEOPLE

Chicken satay served with peanut
  sauce and cucumber relish

Stir-fried mixed vegetables

Spicy minced duck

Massaman beef curry

Hot and sour soup with seafood

Boiled jasmine rice

Watermelon sorbet

BUFFET MENU FOR 20 PEOPLE

Vegetable curry in filo parcels

Thai dim sum served with chilli
  and lime sauce

Green papaya and lime salad

Spicy sliced steak

Hot and sour vermicelli with prawns

Fishcakes with green beans served
  with cucumber relish

Fried rice with prawns, crab
  and curry powder

Fresh egg noodles with mixed
  vegetables

Fresh fruit platter

BASIC RECIPES

At the heart of Thai cooking are the curry pastes, sauces, stocks, relishes and rice dishes, a selection of which are included here. Stock will keep well in the refrigerator for 2–3 days or for 2 months in sealed food containers in the freezer.

BEEF STOCK

INGREDIENTS 1.8 litres (3 pints) cold water | 400 g (13 oz) beef or veal bones with some meat on, roughly chopped | 1 carrot, roughly chopped | 1 celery stick, roughly chopped | 1 onion, quartered | 2.5 cm (1 inch) fresh root ginger, peeled and sliced | 2 coriander plants, including roots | 5 black peppercorns, crushed

ONE Put all the ingredients in a large saucepan and bring to the boil. Reduce the heat and simmer for 1½ hours. From time to time skim off any fat that rises to the surface. **TWO** Strain the stock into a clean bowl, discard the solids and other unwanted parts and leave to cool. **THREE** Put the stock in the refrigerator for 4–5 hours or overnight. Remove any fat that has solidified on the surface and use as required.

Makes about 900 ml (1½ pints)

CHICKEN STOCK

INGREDIENTS 1.8 litres (3 pints) water | 250 g (8 oz) chicken drumsticks, wings and giblets, well rinsed | 1 carrot, peeled and roughly chopped | 1 celery stick, roughly chopped | 1 onion, quartered | 2.5 cm (1 inch) fresh root ginger, peeled and sliced | 2 coriander plants, including roots | 5 peppercorns, crushed

ONE Put all the ingredients in a large saucepan and bring to the boil. Reduce the heat to between medium and low and simmer for 1½ hours. From time to time skim off any fat that rises to the surface. **TWO** Transfer the stock into a clean bowl and leave it to cool. **THREE** Remove the chicken pieces and reserve them for later use, and discard the other solids. **FOUR** Put the stock in the refrigerator for 4–5 hours or overnight. Remove any fat that has solidified on the surface and use as required.

Makes about 900 ml (1½ pints)

VEGETABLE STOCK

INGREDIENTS 1.2 litres (2 pints) cold water | 1 carrot, roughly chopped | 1 celery stick, roughly chopped | 1 onion, quartered | 125 g (4 oz) Chinese white lettuce | 1 cm (½ inch) fresh root ginger, peeled and sliced | 2 whole coriander plants, including roots | 5 peppercorns, crushed

ONE Put all the ingredients in a large saucepan and bring to the boil over high heat. When the water starts to boil reduce the heat to between medium and low and simmer for 30 minutes. Skim from time to time as necessary. **TWO** Strain the stock into a clean bowl and use as required.

Makes about 900 ml (1½ pints)

SEAFOOD STOCK

INGREDIENTS 1.2 litres (2 pints) cold water | 1 carrot, peeled and roughly chopped | 1 celery stick, roughly chopped | 1 onion, quartered | 2 coriander plants, including roots | 200 g (7 oz) fish heads, tail and bones or prawn heads, shells and tails | 5 black peppercorns, crushed

ONE Put the water, carrot, celery, onion and coriander in a large saucepan and heat for 10 minutes or until boiling. **TWO** Add the fish heads, tail and bones or prawn heads and shells and the peppercorns and continue simmering over medium to low heat for another 10–15 minutes, skimming from time to time. **THREE** Strain the stock into a clean bowl, discard the solids and unwanted parts, and leave it to cool. **FOUR** Put the stock in the refrigerator and use as required.

Makes about 600 ml (1 pint)

MASSAMAN CURRY PASTE

INGREDIENTS 2 dried, long red chillies, each about 12 cm (5 inches) long, or 4 dried, small red chillies, each about 5 cm (2 inches) long | 1 lemon grass stalk (white part only), about 12 cm (5 inches) long, finely sliced | 2.5 cm (1 inch) fresh galangal, peeled and finely sliced | 5 kaffir lime leaves, finely chopped | 4 garlic cloves, roughly chopped | 3 shallots, roughly chopped | 4 coriander roots, finely chopped | 1 teaspoon shrimp paste | 1 teaspoon ground allspice | 1 tablespoon paprika | ¼ teaspoon ground white pepper

ONE Remove the stems and slit the chillies lengthways with a sharp knife. Discard all the seeds and roughly chop the flesh. Soak it in hot water for 2 minutes or until it is soft, then drain. **TWO** Use a pestle and mortar or blender to grind the chillies, lemon grass, galangal and kaffir lime leaves into a paste. **THREE** Add the garlic, shallots and coriander root and pound together. **FOUR** Add the remaining ingredients and pound until the mixture becomes a smooth paste.

Makes about 80 g (3 oz)

YELLOW CURRY PASTE

INGREDIENTS 2–3 dried, long red chillies, each about 12 cm (5 inches) long, or 5 dried, small red chillies, each about 5 cm (2 inches) long │ 2 lemon grass stalks (white part only), about 12 cm (5 inches) long, finely sliced │ 2 garlic cloves, roughly chopped │ 3 shallots, roughly chopped │ 1 tablespoon yellow curry powder │ 1 teaspoon ground coriander │ 1 teaspoon ground cumin

ONE Remove the stems and slit the chillies lengthways with a sharp knife. Discard all the seeds and roughly chop the flesh. Soak it in hot water for 2 minutes or until it is soft, then drain. **TWO** Use a pestle and mortar or blender to grind the chillies and lemon grass into a smooth paste. **THREE** Add the garlic and shallots and then the remaining ingredients. Pound together until the mixture becomes a smooth paste.

Makes about 80 g (3 oz)

GREEN CURRY PASTE

INGREDIENTS 4–5 small green chillies, each about 5 cm (2 inches) long │ 1 lemon grass stalk (white part only), about 12 cm (5 inches) long, finely sliced │ 2.5 cm (1 inch) fresh galangal, peeled and finely sliced │ 5 kaffir lime leaves, finely chopped │ 4 garlic cloves, roughly chopped │ 3 shallots, roughly chopped │ 5 coriander roots, finely chopped │ half handful of Thai sweet basil leaves, roughly chopped │ half handful of coriander leaves, roughly chopped │ 1 teaspoon shrimp paste │ 1 teaspoon ground coriander │ 1 teaspoon ground cumin │ ¼ teaspoon ground white pepper

ONE Remove the stems from the chillies. Use a pestle and mortar or blender to grind the chillies, lemon grass, galangal and kaffir lime leaves into a paste. **TWO** Add the garlic, shallots, coriander roots, basil and coriander leaves and grind them together. **THREE** Add the remaining ingredients and grind together until the mixture becomes a smooth paste.

Makes about 125 g (4 oz)

DRY CURRY PASTE

INGREDIENTS 2 dried, long red chillies, each about 12 cm (5 inches) long, or 3 dried, small red chillies, each about 5 cm (2 inches) long | 1 lemon grass stalk (white part only), about 12 cm (5 inches) long, finely sliced | 2.5 cm (1 inch) fresh galangal, peeled and finely sliced | 5 kaffir lime leaves, finely chopped | 4 garlic cloves, roughly chopped | 3 shallots, roughly chopped | 5 coriander roots, finely chopped | 1 teaspoon shrimp paste | 1 tablespoon paprika | 1 teaspoon ground cumin

ONE Remove the stems and slit the chillies lengthways with a sharp knife. Discard all the seeds and roughly chop the flesh. Soak it in hot water for 2 minutes or until it is soft, then drain. **TWO** Use a pestle and mortar or blender to grind the chillies, lemon grass, galangal and kaffir lime leaves into a paste. **THREE** Add the garlic, shallots and coriander roots and grind until smooth. **FOUR** Add the remaining ingredients and grind together until the mixture forms a smooth paste.

Makes about 75 g (3 oz)

RED CURRY PASTE

INGREDIENTS 3–4 dried, long red chillies, each about 12 cm (5 inches) long, or 8 dried, small red chillies, each about 5 cm (2 inches) long | 1 lemon grass stalk (white part only), about 12 cm (5 inches) long, finely sliced | 2.5 cm (1 inch) fresh galangal, peeled and finely sliced | 5 kaffir lime leaves, finely chopped | 4 garlic cloves, roughly chopped | 3 shallots, roughly chopped | 5 coriander roots, finely chopped | 2 teaspoons shrimp paste | 1 teaspoon ground coriander | 1 tablespoon paprika

ONE Remove the stems and slit the chillies lengthways with a sharp knife. Discard all the seeds and roughly chop the flesh. Soak it in hot water for 2 minutes or until it is soft, then drain. **TWO** Use a pestle and mortar or blender to grind the chillies, lemon grass, galangal and kaffir lime leaves into a paste. **THREE** Add the garlic, shallots and coriander roots and grind together. **FOUR** Add the remaining ingredients and grind until the mixture forms a smooth paste.

Makes about 125 g (4 oz)

PEANUT SAUCE

INGREDIENTS 150 g (5 oz) peanuts | 1 tablespoon sunflower oil | 200 ml (7 fl oz) can unsweetened coconut milk, shaken well | 200 ml (7 fl oz) Vegetable Stock *(see page 18)* or water | 2 tablespoons Tamarind Purée *(see page 33)* or lemon juice | 2 tablespoons palm or coconut sugar | 1 tablespoon fish sauce | 15 g (½ oz) dried breadcrumbs

CHILLI PASTE 2 dried, long red chillies, about 12 cm (5 inches) long | 1 lemon grass stalk (white part only), about 10 cm (4 inches) long, finely sliced | 3 garlic cloves, roughly chopped | 2 shallots, roughly chopped | 3 coriander roots, finely chopped | 3 kaffir lime leaves, finely chopped

ONE Dry-fry the peanuts for 8–10 minutes, shaking the pan frequently. Peel when cool and roughly chop. **TWO** Make the paste. Prepare the chillies as for the curry pastes *(see page 23)*. **THREE** Use a pestle and mortar or blender to grind the chillies, lemon grass and garlic. Add the shallots, coriander roots and kaffir lime leaves and grind to a smooth paste. **FOUR** Heat the oil in a nonstick saucepan and stir-fry the chilli paste over medium heat for 1–2 minutes. **FIVE** Add the coconut milk, stock, tamarind purée or lemon juice, sugar and fish sauce and simmer for 4–5 minutes. **SIX** Add the breadcrumbs and peanuts, stir thoroughly and serve with Chicken Satay *(see page 50)*.

Makes sufficient quantity for Chicken Satay

GARLIC AND CHILLI SAUCE

INGREDIENTS 3 small, red and green chillies, lightly crushed | 4 garlic cloves, finely chopped | 2 tablespoons lemon juice | 1 tablespoon light soy sauce

ONE Mix all the ingredients in a small bowl. **TWO** Set aside and serve instead of Ginger and Chilli Sauce with Spring Rolls *(see page 66)*.

Makes 75 ml (3 fl oz)

HOT CHILLI FLAKE SAUCE

INGREDIENTS 2 tablespoons lime or lemon juice | 1 tablespoon light soy sauce | 1½ teaspoons chilli flakes or powder

ONE Mix together all the ingredients in a small bowl. **TWO** Serve with dishes such as Steamed Crabs *(see page 49)*.

Makes 75 ml (3 fl oz)

CUCUMBER RELISH

INGREDIENTS 150 ml (¼ pint) white rice vinegar | 2 teaspoons sugar | ¼ teaspoon salt | 10 cm (4 inches) cucumber, peeled, quartered and finely sliced | 1 small carrot, peeled, quartered and finely sliced | 1 shallot, finely sliced | 1 long red chilli, stemmed, deseeded and finely sliced

ONE In a small saucepan boil the vinegar, sugar and salt until the sugar has dissolved. Leave to cool. **TWO** Pour the liquid over the cucumber, carrot, shallot and chillies. Let it soak through for 30 minutes before serving with Chicken Satay *(see page 50)* or Pan-fried Fishcakes *(see page 56)*.

Makes sufficient quantity for Chicken Satay and Pan-fried Fishcakes

SESAME OIL SAUCE

INGREDIENTS 1 teaspoon sesame seeds │ ½ teaspoon sesame oil │ 1 tablespoon Vegetable Stock *(see page 18)* **or water** │ 1 tablespoon light soy sauce

ONE Dry-fry the sesame seeds in a small pan for 1–2 minutes or until they are lightly browned. Allow to cool down for 5 minutes. **TWO** Use a spoon to try to mash and break some of the sesame seeds to release the flavour. **THREE** Mix the seeds with all the remaining ingredients, and it is ready to serve.

Makes 50 ml (2 fl oz)

CHILLI AND LIME SAUCE

INGREDIENTS 1 long red chilli or 3–4 small chillies, stemmed and finely sliced | 2 garlic cloves, finely chopped | 3 tablespoons lime or lemon juice | 1 teaspoon fish sauce

ONE Mix all the ingredients in a small bowl. **TWO** Serve with dishes such as Thai Dim Sum *(see page 54)*.

Makes 125 ml (4 fl oz)

GINGER AND CHILLI SAUCE

INGREDIENTS 50 g (2 oz) fresh root ginger, peeled | 1 tablespoon Vegetable Stock *(see page 18)* or water | 1 tablespoon light soy sauce | ½ long red chilli, deseeded and finely chopped

ONE Grate the ginger and squeeze it well to yield 1 tablespoon juice. **TWO** Mix the juice together with all the other ingredients in a bowl, and the sauce is ready to serve.

Makes 50 ml (2 fl oz)

TAMARIND PURÉE

INGREDIENTS 50 g (2 oz) dried tamarind pulp | 10 tablespoons boiling hot water

ONE Put the tamarind pulp in a bowl and soak it with the boiling water for 8–10 minutes.

TWO Mash the pulp with a spoon or fork to help it dissolve. Strain the thick liquid into a small, clean bowl and discard the fibres and seeds.

Makes 6–7 tablespoons

STEAMED STICKY RICE

INGREDIENTS 500 g (1 lb) sticky rice

ONE Soak the rice in a bowl of water for at least 3 hours. **TWO** Drain the rice and transfer it to a bamboo basket lined with a double thickness of muslin. Spread the rice in the steamer. **THREE** Bring the water in a pan or wok to a rolling boil and, taking care not to burn your hand, set the bamboo basket over the water. Reduce the heat, cover and steam for 20–25 minutes or until the rice swells and is glistening and tender. Check and replenish the water as necessary every 10 minutes or so. **FOUR** When the rice is cooked, tip it onto a tray and spread it out to cool quickly so that it does not become soggy.

Serves 4

BOILED JASMINE RICE

INGREDIENTS 500 g (1 lb) jasmine rice │ 500 ml (17 fl oz) water at room temperature (use more if necessary)

ONE Place the jasmine rice in a bowl with clean water. Scoop the rice through with your fingers 4–5 times and drain it. Transfer the rice to a saucepan and add the water. **TWO** Cook over high heat, stirring the rice frequently, until the water is boiling. Turn down the heat as low as possible and cover, leaving a small gap between the lid and the side of the pan. **THREE** Simmer gently for 10–15 minutes or until the water has been absorbed. **FOUR** Remove from the heat and leave to stand for another 10 minutes. Remove the lid and stir the rice gently with a rice paddle to fluff and separate the grains. Serve immediately.

Serves 4

BOILED THAI BROWN RICE

INGREDIENTS 500 g (1 lb) Thai brown rice | 900 ml (1½ pints) water at room temperature (use more if necessary)

ONE Place the brown rice in a bowl with clean water. Scoop the rice through with your fingers 4–5 times and drain. Transfer the rice to a saucepan and add the water. **TWO** Cook over high heat, stirring the rice frequently, until the water is boiling. Turn down the heat as low as possible and cover, leaving a small gap between the lid and the side of the pan. **THREE** Simmer gently for 25-30 minutes or until the water has been absorbed. (Check that no water remains at the bottom of the saucepan.) **FOUR** Remove from the heat and let the rice stand for another 10 minutes. Remove the lid and stir the rice gently with a rice paddle to separate the grains. Serve immediately.

Serves 4

SOUPS AND

STARTERS

GOLDEN BASKETS

Golden baskets are a wonderful starter. They are attractive to look at and simple to make. You can find frozen spring roll sheets in oriental super-markets, and the other basic ingredients are widely available. The baskets can be made the day before they are needed and stored in an airtight container. Spoon the filling into the baskets 30 minutes before serving.

INGREDIENTS 200 g (7 oz) pack of spring roll sheets, 12 x 12 cm (5 x 5 inches), or filo pastry, thawed if frozen

FILLING 1–1½ tablespoons sunflower oil | 2 garlic cloves, finely chopped | 200 g (7 oz) minced chicken or prawns | 25 g (1 oz) carrots, finely diced | 25 g (1 oz) sweetcorn kernels, thawed if frozen | 25 g (1 oz) petits pois, thawed if frozen | 50 g (2 oz) red pepper, deseeded and finely diced | 1 tablespoon light soy sauce | ½ teaspoon ground white pepper | pinch of curry powder | 1 spring onion, finely chopped

TO SERVE 30 coriander leaves | 2 long red chillies, stemmed, deseeded and finely sliced

ONE Make the filling. Heat the oil in a nonstick wok or frying pan and stir-fry the garlic over medium heat until it is lightly browned. Add the chicken or prawns, crumbling and breaking up the meat until it has separated and cooked. **TWO** Add the carrots, sweetcorn, petits pois and red pepper and stir-fry for 1–2 minutes. Add the soy sauce, ground white pepper, curry powder and spring onion, combine well and set aside. **THREE** Cut the spring roll sheets or filo pastry into 60 squares, each 6 x 6 cm (2½ x 2½ inches). Lay 2 squares in each indentation in a cake tin used for making 3.5 cm (1½ inch) cakes, overlapping the squares so that the top sheet is at an angle of 45 degrees to the bottom one. Prepare 30 baskets and bake in a preheated oven, 180°C (350°F), Gas Mark 4, for 10–12 minutes or until they are crispy and golden brown. Carefully remove the baskets and allow them to cool slightly. **FOUR** Spoon the filling into the baskets and serve at room temperature, garnished with a coriander leaf and some slices of chilli.

Makes 30 baskets; serves 4–6 as a starter

NUTRIENT ANALYSIS PER BASKET 153 kJ – 37 kcal – 2 g protein – 5 g carbohydrate – 0 g sugars – 1 g fat – 0 g saturates – 0 g fibre – 40 mg sodium

recipe illustrated on pages 44–45

VEGETABLE CURRY IN FILO PARCELS

I use filo pastry for these curry triangles and bake them in the oven rather than deep-frying them as I would curry puffs.

INGREDIENTS 1 tablespoon sunflower oil | 2–3 garlic cloves, finely chopped | 15 g (½ oz) coriander roots (about 2 roots), finely chopped | 1 cm (½ inch) fresh root ginger, peeled and finely chopped | 1 onion, finely chopped | 50 g (2 oz) carrot, finely diced | 50 g (2 oz) red pepper, deseeded and finely diced | 50 g (2 oz) sweetcorn kernels, thawed if frozen | 50 g (2 oz) petits pois, thawed if frozen | 500 g (1 lb) potatoes, boiled in their skins and cut into small dice | 1½ tablespoons light soy sauce | 1 teaspoon curry powder | pinch of ground white pepper | ¼ long red chilli, stemmed, deseeded and finely sliced (optional) | 2 x 275 g (9 oz) packs filo sheets, thawed if frozen | 2–3 tablespoons sunflower oil, for brushing

ONE Heat the oil in a nonstick wok or frying pan and stir-fry the garlic over medium heat until it is lightly browned. Add the coriander, ginger and onion and cook over medium heat for 1–2 minutes. **TWO** Add the carrot, red pepper, sweetcorn and petits pois and stir-fry for a further 2–3 minutes. **THREE** Stir in the potatoes, soy sauce, curry powder, ground white pepper and chilli (if used). Leave to cool to room temperature. **FOUR** Meanwhile, cut 20 filo pastry strips, each 12 x 25 cm (5 x 10 inches). Place 3 filo strips with the short sides nearest you in front of you and keep the remaining sheets in a plastic bag to prevent them from drying out. **FIVE** Put 2 tablespoons of the filling on the bottom left-hand corner of the pastry. Fold up the corner to make a triangle and continue to flip the triangle along the length of the filo strip to wrap the filling in the pastry. **SIX** Place the filo triangle on a lightly oiled baking sheet. Repeat with the remaining filling and filo rectangles, placing them on the baking sheet so that there is a slight gap between each one. Brush each triangle with a little oil. **SEVEN** Bake the parcels in a preheated oven, 180°C (350°F), Gas Mark 4, for 5 minutes. Turn them upside down and bake for another 2–3 minutes or until crispy and golden brown. Serve warm or at room temperature.

Makes 20; serves 6–8 as a starter

NUTRIENT ANALYSIS PER SERVING 1858 kJ – 444 kcal – 12 g protein – 76 g carbohydrate – 4 g sugars – 11 g fat – 1 g saturates – 3 g fibre – 470 mg sodium

HEALTHY TIP Unlike most other types of pastry, filo contains little fat. In 100 g (3½ oz) filo pastry there are just 2 g of fat and 300 kcal. The same weight of shortcrust pastry contains 29 g fat and 449 kcal.

STEAMED CRABS

A seaside favourite, and much esteemed in Thailand, steamed crabs make a lovely starter to a Thai meal. Serve with Hot Chilli Flake Sauce *(see page 28)* or Ginger and Chilli Sauce *(see page 32)*.

INGREDIENTS 2 kg (4 lb) fresh, uncooked crabs (3–4 crabs)

ONE Prepare the crabs *(see page 10)*. **TWO** Fill a wok or steamer pan with water. Insert the bamboo steamer basket or steamer rack, cover the wok and bring the water to boiling point over a high heat. **THREE** Place the crabs on a baking dish that will fit on the rack of the bamboo steamer basket but that is slightly larger than the crabs. **FOUR** Taking care not to burn your hand, set the dish inside the steamer basket and simmer for 20–25 minutes or until the crabs are cooked. Check and replenish the water every 10 minutes or so. **FIVE** Remove the crabs from the steamer and serve them hot or warm.

Serves 4 as a starter

NUTRIENT ANALYSIS PER SERVING 547 kJ – 130 kcal – 20 g protein – 1 g carbohydrate – 0 g sugars – 5 g fat – 1 g saturates – 0 g fibre – 370 mg sodium

HEALTHY TIP Crab is an excellent source of protein and is low in fat and calories. It also supplies zinc, copper, calcium, magnesium and iron.

CHICKEN SATAY

Satay consists of skewers of meat – chicken as here, or beef, lamb, turkey or a combination of these – marinated in coconut milk and spices, and grilled quickly over charcoal. Originating in Indonesia, this tasty dish has travelled north up the peninsula, becoming adapted to suit local taste. You will need 40 bamboo skewers, each 18–20 cm (7–8 inches) long. Soak them in water for about an hour before you use them so that they do not burn during cooking. Serve hot with Peanut Sauce *(see page 26)* and Cucumber Relish *(see page 29)*.

INGREDIENTS 1 kg (2 lb) chicken breasts

MARINADE 2 shallots, roughly chopped │ 3 garlic cloves, roughly chopped │ 4 coriander roots, finely chopped │ 2.5 cm (1 inch) fresh root ginger, peeled and sliced │ 1 tablespoon ground coriander │ 1 tablespoon ground cumin │ 1 tablespoon ground turmeric │ 1 teaspoon curry powder │ 1½ tablespoons light soy sauce │ 2 tablespoons sunflower oil │ 200 ml (7 fl oz) can unsweetened coconut milk, well stirred │ 150 ml (¼ pint) Chicken Stock *(see page 17)* or water │ 1 tablespoon palm or coconut sugar

ONE Cut the chicken into pieces 3.5 x 10 cm (1½ x 4 inches) and 5 mm (¼ inch) thick and put them in a mixing bowl. **TWO** Make the marinade. Use a pestle and mortar or food processor to blend the shallots, garlic, coriander root and ginger into a paste and add the mixture to the chicken together with the remaining marinade ingredients. Mix thoroughly with a spoon or your fingers. Cover with clingfilm and refrigerate for at least 5 hours or overnight, turning the chicken occasionally. **THREE** Thread a piece of the marinated chicken on to each presoaked bamboo skewer as if you were sewing a piece of material. (Use 2 pieces on each stick if they are small.) **FOUR** Preheat the barbecue or a foil-lined grill to high heat and cook the satay sticks for 5–7 minutes on each side or until they are cooked through and slightly charred. Turn frequently and brush the marinade sauce over the meat during cooking.

Makes 40 sticks; serves 6–8 as a starter

NUTRIENT ANALYSIS PER SERVING 1306 kJ – 312 kcal – 38 g protein – 7 g carbohydrate – 5 g sugars – 5 g fat – 6 g saturates – 0 g fibre – 160 mg sodium

HEALTHY TIP The white meat of a chicken is lower in calories, lower in fat and higher in protein than dark meat. Use free-range or organic chicken for the best flavour.

recipe illustrated on pages 52–53

THAI DIM SUM

Originating in China, dim sum has long been enjoyed in Thailand where it is often eaten as a substantial snack. It also makes an excellent starter to a larger meal. Serve with Chilli and Lime Sauce *(see page 31)*.

INGREDIENTS about 30 yellow won ton sheets or wrappers, each 8 x 8 cm (3 x 3 inches) | sunflower oil, for brushing

FILLING 300 g (10 oz) minced prawns | 125 g (4 oz) can crab meat, drained | 75 g (3 oz) can water chestnuts, drained and roughly chopped | 2 garlic cloves, finely chopped | 2 spring onions (white part only), finely sliced | 1 tablespoon oyster sauce | 1 tablespoon soy sauce | 1 teaspoon sesame oil | ⅛ teaspoon ground white pepper

TO SERVE 30 coriander leaves | ¼ long red chilli, stemmed, deseeded and finely sliced

ONE Make the filling. Mix all the ingredients together in a mixing bowl. **TWO** Spoon about 1 tablespoon of the mixture into the middle of each won ton sheet. Pull up the sheet to form a bag but leave an opening about 1 cm (½ inch) wide at the top so that the filling is not entirely covered. **THREE** Fill a wok or a steamer pan with water, place the bamboo steamer basket or steamer rack over the water, cover and place over high heat. Brush a plate with a little sunflower oil and place the dim sum on it, making sure they are closely packed. Set the plate inside the steamer basket carefully and simmer for 10 minutes over medium heat. (You will probably need to repeat the cooking process two or three times.) **FOUR** To serve, garnish the top of each dim sum with a coriander leaf and some chilli slices.

Makes 30; serves 4–6 as a starter

NUTRIENT ANALYSIS PER SERVING 1380 kJ – 330 kcal – 22 g protein – 36 g carbohydrate – 1 g sugars – 11 g fat – 1 g saturates – 0 g fibre – 970 mg sodium

PAN-FRIED FISHCAKES

Thai fishcakes are especially popular outside Thailand, but they are not always made with the right blend of flavours. Here is an authentic Thai recipe for you to enjoy. If you do not have time to make the chilli paste, you can use 1 tablespoon of bought red curry paste instead. Serve with **Cucumber Relish** *(see page 29)*.

INGREDIENTS 500 g (1 lb) white fish fillet, skinned, cleaned and roughly chopped | 1 tablespoon fish sauce | 1½ tablespoons cornflour | 1 egg | 50 g (2 oz) green beans, finely sliced | 5 kaffir lime leaves, finely sliced | sunflower oil for frying

CHILLI PASTE 2 dried, long red chillies, each about 12 cm (5 inches) long | 1 lemon grass stalk (white part only), 8 cm (3 inches) long, finely sliced | 3 garlic cloves, roughly chopped | 2 shallots, roughly chopped | 2 coriander roots, cleaned and finely chopped

ONE Make the chilli paste. Remove the stems and slit the chillies lengthways with a sharp knife. Discard the seeds. Roughly chop the flesh, soak it in hot water for 2 minutes or until it is soft, then drain. **TWO** Use a pestle and mortar to pound the chillies, lemon grass, garlic, shallots and coriander roots until the mixture forms a smooth paste. **THREE** Use a food processor or a blender to mince the fish fillets. Add the chilli paste (or red curry paste), fish sauce, cornflour and egg and blend briefly until smooth. Spoon the mixture into a bowl and mix with the green beans and kaffir lime leaves. **FOUR** Use a tablespoon or damp hands to shape the fish mixture into thin, flat cakes, 5 cm (2 inches) across, and put them on a baking sheet lined with greaseproof paper while you use all the mixture. **FIVE** Heat a little sunflower oil in a nonstick frying pan and gently fry 8–10 fishcakes at a time (depending on size of your frying pan), making sure there is a slight gap between each one. Fry for 2–3 minutes on each side or until cooked and lightly browned. Add a little oil to the pan before cooking each batch.

Makes 25–30; serves 6–8 as a starter

NUTRIENT ANALYSIS PER FISHCAKE 159 kJ – 38 kcal – 4 g protein – 2 g carbohydrate – 0 g sugars – 2 g fat – 0 g saturates – 0 g fibre – 54 mg sodium

HEALTHY TIP These pan-fried fishcakes are a much healthier alternative to the usual deep-fried version.

Check amount of Cornflour
Quite a wet mixture
Breaks ups slightly

recipe illustrated on pages 58–59

DRY WON TON

This is a popular one-meal dish in noodle restaurants. There are two types of won ton: those that are served in soups, and those, as here, that are served in various dry dishes.

INGREDIENTS 40 won ton sheets or wrappers, 8 x 8 cm (3 x 3 inches) │ 300 g (10 oz) raw prawns │ 1½ tablespoons sunflower oil │ 4–5 garlic cloves, finely chopped │ 250 g (8 oz) Chinese cabbage (cho sum) or spinach leaves, roughly chopped │ 250 g (8 oz) fresh bean sprouts, tails removed │ 2 tablespoons light soy sauce │ 1 tablespoon preserved radish (optional)

FILLING 500 g (1 lb) minced prawns, pork or chicken │ 4 garlic cloves, finely chopped │ 4 coriander roots, finely chopped │ ¼ teaspoon ground white pepper

TO SERVE 125 g (4 oz) cooked crab claws (about 8 claws) or cooked crab meat │ 2 spring onions, finely sliced diagonally │ ground white pepper

ONE Make the filling. Combine the minced prawns or meat with the garlic, coriander roots and ground white pepper. **TWO** Spoon a little of the mixture into the middle of each won ton sheet. Brush the edges with water and gather up the sheet, squeezing the corners together to make a little purse. **THREE** Prepare the prawns *(see page 11)*. **FOUR** Heat the oil in a nonstick wok or frying pan and stir-fry the garlic over medium heat until it is lightly browned. Transfer to a small bowl. **FIVE** Cook the Chinese cabbage in boiling water for 1–2 minutes. Use a sieve or coarse-meshed strainer to drain the leaves, then put them into a mixing bowl. **SIX** Cook the prawns in boiling water for 1–2 minutes or until they open and turn pink. Drain and put them in the mixing bowl. **SEVEN** Gently drop each won ton purse into the boiling water and cook for 2–3 minutes or until the prawn inside is cooked. Drain and put into the mixing bowl. Add the bean sprouts, garlic oil, soy sauce and preserved radish (if used) and toss together. Spoon the mixture into 4 individual serving bowls, season with ground white pepper and serve immediately with crab claws and spring onions.

Serves 4 as a main dish

NUTRIENT ANALYSIS PER SERVING 1645 kJ – 396 kcal – 34 g protein – 48 g carbohydrate – 2 g sugars – 7 g fat – 1 g saturates – 0 g fibre – 719 mg sodium

HEALTHY TIP Bean sprouts are a good source of vitamin C and also contain small amounts of the B-group vitamins as well as potassium and iron.

BARBECUED PORK SPARE RIBS

We can eat outside in Thailand at any time of the year, so we have lots of barbecues. Everyone loves this tasty dish, especially children, and it can be served as a starter or as finger food at a party. If possible, ask your butcher to prepare baby back ribs for you.

INGREDIENTS 1 kg (2 lb) pork spare ribs, cut into 10–12 cm (4–5 inches) lengths │ 3 garlic cloves, finely chopped │ 3 coriander roots, cleaned and finely chopped, or 1 teaspoon ground coriander │ 2 tablespoons clear honey │ 2 tablespoons tomato ketchup │ 1 tablespoon light soy sauce │ ½ teaspoon ground white pepper │ ¼ teaspoon ground allspice (optional)

TO SERVE 1 red chilli, finely sliced │ 1 spring onion, finely sliced

ONE In a large mixing bowl combine all the ingredients with your fingers or a spoon. Cover with clingfilm and leave for at least 3 hours or, if time allows, overnight in the refrigerator. **TWO** Place the ribs with all the marinade in a baking dish and cook in a preheated oven, 180°C (350°F), Gas Mark 4, for 45 minutes to 1 hour, basting several times during cooking. Grill for a further 5 minutes on each side until well browned and slightly charred. **THREE** Alternatively, preheat the barbecue or foil-lined grill to medium heat and put the grill rack into the tray. Grill the pork, turning several times and brushing frequently with the remaining sauce until the meat is cooked through and slightly charred, which should take 10–12 minutes on each side. Serve garnished with chilli and spring onion.

Serves 4 as a starter

NUTRIENT ANALYSIS PER SERVING 1215 kJ – 290 kcal – 23 g protein – 14 g carbohydrate – 14 g sugars – 16 g fat – 6 g saturates – 0 g fibre – 320 mg sodium

HEALTHY TIP Honey is good source of glucose and fructose and can therefore help to reduce fatigue after a strenuous workout.

recipe illustrated on pages 64–65

SPRING ROLLS

These savoury rolls are popular throughout Southeast Asia. The Thai version is a delicate cross between Chinese and Vietnamese styles. Instead of being deep-fried, the rolls are wrapped with sheets of filo pastry and baked in the oven until they are golden and crispy. Serve with Ginger and Chilli Sauce *(see page 32)* or Sesame Oil Sauce *(see page 30).*

INGREDIENTS 125 g (4 oz) vermicelli or dried wun sen noodles │ 15 g (½ oz) dried black fungus │ 1 tablespoon sunflower oil, plus extra for brushing │ 3–4 garlic cloves, finely chopped │ 150 g (5 oz) fresh bean sprouts │ 50 g (2 oz) carrots, finely grated │ 50 g (2 oz) petits pois, thawed if frozen │ 50 g (2 oz) sweetcorn kernels, thawed if frozen │ 1 cm (½ inch) fresh root ginger, peeled and finely grated │ 2 tablespoons light soy sauce │ ¼ teaspoon ground white pepper │ 3 x 275 g (9 oz) packets filo pastry, thawed if frozen

ONE Soak the noodles in hot water for 1–2 minutes or until they are soft. Drain and cut them into small pieces. Soak the dried black fungus in hot water for 2–3 minutes or until it is soft. Drain and chop it finely. **TWO** Heat the oil in a nonstick wok or frying pan and stir-fry the garlic over medium heat until it is lightly browned. Add the noodles, dried black fungus, bean sprouts, carrots, petits pois, sweetcorn, ginger, soy sauce and ground white pepper. Cook for another 4 5 minutes and leave to cool. **THREE** Cut 50 filo pastry squares, each 10 x 10 cm (4 x 4 inches). **FOUR** Keep the remaining filo in a plastic bag to prevent the squares from drying out while you work. Place 2 filo squares on the work surface and spoon 2 teaspoons of the filling along the side nearest to you and about 2.5 cm (1 inch) from the edge. Bring the edge up, then roll it away from you, half a turn over the filling. Fold the sides into the centre to enclose the filling, then wrap and seal the join tightly. Repeat until you have used all the filling and filo squares. Place the spring rolls join side down on a lightly greased baking sheet, making sure there is a slight gap between each one, and brush each one with a little oil. **FIVE** Bake in a preheated oven, 180°C (350°F), Gas Mark 4, for 5 minutes. Turn upside down, bake for another 2–3 minutes or until crispy and golden brown. Serve warm or at room temperature.

Makes 50; serves 10–15 as a starter

NUTRIENT ANALYSIS PER SPRING ROLL 290 kJ – 69 kcal – 2 g protein – 13 g carbohydrate – 0 g sugars – 1 g fat – 0 g saturates   0 g fibre – 85 mg sodium

HEALTHY TIP Frozen vegetables often contain more vitamin C than fresh vegetables. Frozen peas, for example, retain 60–70 per cent of their vitamin C content after freezing.

GRILLED SEAFOOD WITH PINEAPPLE

INGREDIENTS 300 g (10 oz) raw prawns or large shrimps | 300 g (10 oz) scallops | 1 fresh pineapple, cut into 25 x 2.5 cm (1 inch) cubes

MARINADE 2 garlic cloves, finely chopped | 1 tablespoon finely chopped coriander leaves | 1 long red chilli, deseeded and finely chopped | 1 tablespoon sesame oil | 1½ tablespoons light soy sauce | ½ teaspoon ground white pepper

ONE Prepare the prawns and scallops *(see page 11)*. **TWO** Put all the marinade ingredients in a mixing bowl. Add the prawns and scallops, mix together thoroughly and marinate for at least 30 minutes. **THREE** Divide the prawns and scallops into separate groups. Thread the prawns and pineapple alternately on to 4 presoaked bamboo sticks. Thread the scallops and more pineapple on to the remaining sticks. **FOUR** Grill them a few inches below a high heat for 8–10 minutes on each side.

Serves 4 as a starter

NUTRIENT ANALYSIS PER SERVING 802 kJ – 189 kcal – 25 g protein – 13 g carbohydrate – 10 g sugars – 5 g fat – 1 g saturates – 1 g fibre – 600 mg sodium

BEAN SPROUTS AND TOFU SOUP

Easy to make, this can be served as either a main dish or a starter. You can use minced prawn instead of chicken or pork, if you prefer. If you cannot find coriander roots, use 1 tablespoon finely chopped coriander leaves instead. Big head bean sprouts, which are available in oriental supermarkets, have much larger heads than the usual type.

INGREDIENTS 10 dried black fungus │ 150 g (5 oz) minced chicken or pork │ 3 garlic cloves, finely chopped │ 2–3 coriander roots, finely chopped │ 150 g (5 oz) big head bean sprouts │ 375 g (12 oz) soft or firm tofu │ 1.8 litres (3 pints) Chicken Stock *(see page 17)* or Vegetable Stock *(see page 18)* │ 2 tablespoons light soy sauce

TO SERVE ground white pepper │ 2 spring onions, finely sliced

ONE Soak the dried black fungus in hot water for 2–3 minutes or until it is soft. Drain and finely chop it. **TWO** In a mixing bowl combine the minced meat, garlic, coriander and dried black fungus. **THREE** Clean the bean sprouts and discard the tails. Drain the tofu and cut it into 2.5 cm (1 inch) cubes. **FOUR** Heat the stock in a saucepan until it is boiling. Add the soy sauce. Use a spoon or wet fingers to shape the minced meat mixture into small balls, about 1 cm (½ inch) across, and gently drop them into the stock. Cook for 2–3 minutes over medium heat. **FIVE** Add the tofu and bean sprouts and simmer for another 2–3 minutes, taking care not to let the tofu cubes lose their shape. Spoon into a serving bowl, season with ground white pepper and serve garnished with spring onions.

Serves 4 with 2 other main dishes

NUTRIENT ANALYSIS PER SERVING 630 kJ – 150 kcal – 18 g protein – 8 g carbohydrate – 0 g sugars – 5 g fat – 1 g saturates – 0 g fibre – 36 mg sodium

HOT AND SOUR SOUP WITH SEAFOOD

INGREDIENTS 625 g (1¼ lb) mixed seafood, such as raw prawns, squid, white fish fillet, scallops and mussels │ 900 ml (1½ pints) Seafood Stock *(see page 19)* │ 3 lemon grass stalks (white part only), each 12 cm (5 inches) long, bruised │ 5 coriander roots, cleaned and bruised │ 2 tablespoons fish sauce │ 125 g (4 oz) straw or mixed mushrooms │ 1 onion, quartered │ 4–5 small red and green chillies, slightly crushed │ 12 cherry tomatoes │ 5 kaffir lime leaves, torn, plus extra, sliced, to garnish │ 3 tablespoons lime or lemon juice

ONE Prepare the mixed seafood *(see pages 10–11)*. **TWO** Put the stock, lemon grass, coriander and fish sauce in a saucepan and heat to boiling point. **THREE** Reduce the heat, add the seafood and cook for 2 minutes. **FOUR** Quarter any large mushrooms and add the mushrooms, onion, chillies, tomatoes, kaffir lime leaves and lime or lemon juice. Cook for another 2–3 minutes, taking care not to let the tomatoes lose their shape. **FIVE** Turn into a serving bowl, garnish with a few sliced kaffir lime leaves and serve.

Serves 4 with 2 other main dishes

NUTRIENT ANALYSIS PER SERVING 660 kJ – 156 kcal – 26 g protein – 8 g carbohydrate – 4 g sugars – 2 g fat – 0 g saturates – 2 g fibre – 830 mg sodium

CHICKEN, COCONUT AND GALANGAL SOUP

Here is a classic Thai dish that is enjoyed by adults and children alike. The galangal and lemon grass give it plenty of flavour, but it is not too hot.

INGREDIENTS 200 ml (7 fl oz) can coconut milk, shaken well │ 200 ml (7 fl oz) Chicken Stock (*see page 17*) │ 2 lemon grass stalks (white part only), each 12 cm (5 inches) long and cut into a tassel or bruised │ 5 cm (2 inches) fresh galangal, peeled and cut into several pieces │ 15 black peppercorns, crushed │ 400 g (13 oz) skinless chicken breast fillets, sliced │ 1½ tablespoons fish sauce │ 1 tablespoon palm or coconut sugar │ 150 g (5 oz) mixed mushrooms, such as oyster, shiitake or button │ 200 g (7 oz) cherry tomatoes (about 16) │ 2½ tablespoons lime or lemon juice │ 5 kaffir lime leaves, torn in half │ 3–5 small red and green chillies, bruised │ coriander leaves, to garnish

ONE Heat the coconut milk, stock, lemon grass, galangal and peppercorns in a saucepan or wok over medium heat and bring to the boil. **TWO** Add the chicken, fish sauce and sugar and, stirring constantly, simmer for 5 minutes or until the chicken is cooked through. **THREE** Halve the mushrooms if they are large and remove and discard the hard stalks. Add the tomatoes and mushrooms and simmer for 2–3 minutes, taking care that the tomatoes do not lose their shape. Add the lime or lemon juice, kaffir lime leaves and chillies for the last few seconds. Serve garnished with a few coriander leaves.

Serves 4 with 2 other main dishes

NUTRIENT ANALYSIS PER SERVING 993 kJ – 237 kcal – 24 g protein – 9 g carbohydrate – 8 g sugars – 12 g fat – 7 g saturates – 2 g fibre – 450 mg sodium

HEALTHY TIP Galangal aids digestion, relieves gastric distress and alleviates the symptoms of morning sickness and motion sickness. It also has antifungal and antibacterial properties.

recipe illustrated on pages 76–77

SOUR MINCED PORK SOUP WITH SNAKE BEANS

In Thailand this slightly hot and sour soup is a popular addition to a main meal. Snake beans are narrow, round and stringless beans, 30–90 cm (12–36 inches) long, and can be found in Thai or oriental supermarkets. Green beans can be used as an alternative if you have trouble finding them. You can also use fish or mixed seafood, which does not need to be minced, instead of meat.

INGREDIENTS 4 dried, long red chillies, about 12 cm (5 inches) long, or 4 dried, small red chillies, about 5 cm (2 inches) long | 7 shallots, roughly chopped | 4 garlic cloves, roughly chopped | 1 teaspoon shrimp paste | 1.2 litres (2 pints) Vegetable Stock *(see page 18)* | 375 g (12 oz) minced pork or chicken | 375 g (12 oz) snake beans, cut into 2.5 cm (1 inch) pieces | 2 tablespoons fish sauce | 5 tablespoons lemon juice

ONE Remove the stems and slit the chillies lengthways with a sharp knife. Discard all the seeds and roughly chop the flesh. Soak it in hot water for 2 minutes or until it is soft, then drain. **TWO** Use a pestle and mortar to pound together the chillies, shallots, garlic and shrimp paste until the mixture forms a smooth paste. **THREE** Put the stock in a saucepan and heat it until it is boiling. Stir in the chilli paste mixture and reduce the heat to medium. **FOUR** Use a spoon or your wet hand to shape the minced meat into small balls, each about 1 cm (½ inch) across, and lower the balls into the stock with the beans, fish sauce and lemon juice. Cook for 4–5 minutes and spoon into a serving bowl.

Serves 4 with 2 other main dishes

NUTRIENT ANALYSIS PER SERVING 809 kJ – 194 kcal – 23 g protein – 8 g carbohydrate – 5 g sugars – 8 g fat – 2 g saturates – 4 g fibre – 90 mg sodium

HEALTHY TIP Fibre adds bulk or roughage to your diet. Snake beans are rich in fibre, but they should not be overcooked.

SALADS

GREEN PAPAYA SALAD WITH CHILLI AND LIME

This crunchy salad is popular all over Thailand. It is mostly a tangle of pale green shreds of unripe papaya. You can also use grated carrots if it is difficult to find green papaya but the taste is not as good. This salad goes well with sticky rice. You will be able to make one serving at a time in your mortar. To serve 4 people, multiply the ingredients by 4 and repeat the process. If you cannot find ready-ground dried shrimps, use whole dried shrimps and grind them before preparing the salad.

INGREDIENTS 125 g (4 oz) small hard, green, unripe papaya | 2 tablespoons lime or lemon juice, plus a small piece of rind | ½ tablespoon fish sauce | ½ tablespoon palm or coconut sugar | 1–2 garlic cloves | 25 g (1 oz) roasted peanuts *(see page 26)* | 25 g (1 oz) green beans, cut into 2.5 cm (1 inch) pieces | ½ tablespoon ground dried shrimp | 1 small red and 1 green chilli | 50 g (2 oz) cherry tomatoes, left whole, or 2 tomatoes, cut into 6 pieces

ONE Use a vegetable peeler to remove the skin from the papaya. Chop the flesh into long, thin shreds or use a grater. Discard any seeds and put the flesh in a bowl. **TWO** Mix the lime or lemon juice with the fish sauce and sugar in a small bowl. **THREE** Pound the garlic into a paste using a large pestle and mortar. Add the roasted peanuts and pound them roughly with the garlic. Add the papaya and pound gently, using a spoon to scrape down the sides, turning and mixing the paste well. Add the beans, dried shrimp and chilli. Keep pounding and turning to bruise the ingredients. **FOUR** Add the sugar mixture, tomatoes and a piece of lime or lemon rind. Mix and lightly pound for another minute until all the ingredients are thoroughly mixed. (As the juice comes out, pound more gently so the liquid doesn't splash.) **FIVE** Spoon the papaya salad on to a serving plate with all of the sauce remaining in the mortar and serve immediately.

Serves 1 as a starter

NUTRIENT ANALYSIS PER SERVING 1215 kJ – 290 kcal – 15 g protein – 28 g carbohydrate – 13 g sugars – 13 g fat – 2 g saturates – 5 g fibre – 910 mg sodium

HEALTHY TIP Green papaya contains papain, an enzyme that has a soothing effect on the stomach and assists in the digestion of protein.

recipe illustrated on pages 86–87

CUCUMBER SALAD WITH CHICKEN THREADS

INGREDIENTS 150 g (5 oz) skinned chicken breasts │ 250 g (8 oz) cucumber, skinned │ 2 shallots, finely sliced │ 15 g (½ oz) roasted peanuts *(see page 26)*, **roughly chopped** │ coriander leaves, to garnish

SALAD DRESSING 1–2 small red chillies, finely chopped │ 3 tablespoons lime or lemon juice │ 1 tablespoon fish sauce

ONE Make the salad dressing. Mix all the ingredients together in a small bowl. This can be done 1–2 hours before it is needed. **TWO** Bring a saucepan of water to the boil. Add the chicken, cook for 5 minutes and drain. Transfer the chicken to a mixing bowl and leave it to cool, then tear it into long, thin threads. **THREE** Discard the seeds and slice the cucumber with a grater into long, thin shreds and mix them with the chicken. **FOUR** Add the shallots, roasted peanuts and salad dressing and combine well. Garnish with a few coriander leaves before serving.

Serves 4 with 2 other main dishes

NUTRIENT ANALYSIS PER SERVING 339 kJ – 80 kcal – 10 g protein – 4 g carbohydrate – 2 g sugars – 3 g fat – 1 g saturates – 1 g fibre – 240 mg sodium

HEALTHY TIP Low in saturated fat, cholesterol and sodium, cucumber is a good source of silica which helps to build healthy connective tissue. It also contains plenty of dietary fibre, together with the water you need when ingesting fibre, plus various trace elements such as copper and manganese.

SPICY SLICED STEAK

When Thai men get together to drink they love to eat this dish, originating from the north of Thailand. Adjust the amount of chilli to suit your taste.

INGREDIENTS 375 g (12 oz) rump, sirloin or fillet steak │ 1 lemon grass stalk (white part only), 12 cm (5 inches) long, finely sliced │ 3 shallots, finely sliced │ 5 kaffir lime leaves, finely sliced │ 4 tablespoons lemon juice │ 1½ tablespoons fish sauce │ 1 tablespoon ground rice (see page 12) │ 3–4 small red or green chillies, finely chopped, or ½–1 teaspoon chilli powder (or to taste) │ 2 tablespoons mint leaves, roughly chopped │ mixed salad leaves

ONE Preheat the barbecue or grill to medium. If you are using a grill, line the tray with foil. Put the beef on the grill rack and cook for 5–7 minutes on each side, turning occasionally. Leave the meat to rest for at least 5 minutes then slice it crossways into strips. **TWO** In a bowl mix together the beef, lemon grass, shallots, kaffir lime leaves, lemon juice, fish sauce, ground rice, chillies or chilli powder and mint leaves. **THREE** Line a serving plate with a few mixed salad leaves and spoon over the sliced steak. Serve immediately.

Serves 4 with 3 other main dishes

NUTRIENT ANALYSIS PER SERVING 694 kJ – 166 kcal – 21 g protein – 7 g carbohydrate – 1 g sugars – 6 g fat – 3 g saturates – 0 g fibre – 360 mg sodium

HEALTHY TIP Few foods are as healthy as fresh salad. For maximum benefits use Cos lettuce for its high-fibre content, vitamin C, beta-carotene and folic acid.

GRILLED SQUID SALAD WITH CASHEW NUTS

Mango and cashew nuts are combined here in this delicious and unusual salad with lightly grilled squid.

INGREDIENTS 1 kg (2 lb) squid | 1 small green mango or cooking apple, skinned and finely shredded | 125 g (4 oz) carrot, finely shredded | 6 shallots, finely sliced | 50 g (2 oz) dry-fried cashew nuts | Little Gem lettuce leaves | coriander leaves, to garnish

SALAD DRESSING 3–4 small red and green chillies, finely chopped | 5 tablespoons lime or lemon juice | 1½ tablespoons fish sauce

ONE Make the salad dressing. Combine all the ingredients in a small bowl. **TWO** Prepare the squid *(see page 11)*. Grill or barbecue the squid for 3–4 minutes on each side, turning occasionally, until they are cooked through. Remove the squid from the heat, transfer to a mixing bowl and leave to cool. **THREE** Mix the mango, carrot, shallots and salad dressing with the squid and combine well. **FOUR** Line a serving plate with lettuce leaves and spoon over the squid. Sprinkle with the cashew nuts, garnish with coriander leaves and serve immediately.

Serves 4 with 3 other main dishes

NUTRIENT ANALYSIS PER SERVING 1250 kJ – 299 kcal – 40 g protein – 13 g carbohydrate – 7 g sugars – 8 g fat – 1 g saturates – 1 g fibre – 460 mg sodium

HEALTHY TIP Cashew nuts are a good source of copper, magnesium, zinc and biotin. Magnesium balances the effects of calcium and helps to regulate nerve and muscle tone.

recipe illustrated on pages 94–95

HOT AND SOUR VERMICELLI WITH PRAWNS

This is a tangy version of a noodle salad. Vermicelli or wun sen noodles are made from mung beans, and they become nearly transparent when they have been soaked in hot water.

INGREDIENTS 175 g (6 oz) large raw prawns | 125 g (4 oz) mung bean vermicelli noodles | 15 g (½ oz) dried black fungus | 3 tablespoons lime or lemon juice | 1 tablespoon fish sauce | 2 lemon grass stalks (white part only), each 12 cm (5 inches) long, finely sliced | 3 shallots, finely sliced | ¼–½ teaspoon chilli powder or 2–3 small red and green chillies, finely sliced (or to taste) | 3 spring onions, finely chopped | mixed salad leaves | mint or coriander leaves, to garnish

ONE Prepare the prawns *(see page 11)*. Soak the noodles in hot water for 1–2 minutes or until they are soft. Drain and roughly chop them. Soak the dried black fungus in hot water for 2–3 minutes or until it is soft. Drain and roughly chop it. **TWO** In a saucepan or wok cook the prawns over medium heat with the lime or lemon juice and fish sauce for 1–2 minutes or until the prawns open and turn pink. **THREE** Add the noodles and dried black fungus and cook for another 2 minutes or until the noodles are cooked. Remove from the heat. **FOUR** Add the lemon grass, shallots, chilli powder or chillies and spring onions and mix well. Line a serving plate with mixed salad leaves and spoon over the seafood mixture. Garnish with a few mint or coriander leaves and serve immediately.

Serves 4 with 2 other main dishes

NUTRIENT ANALYSIS PER SERVING 640 kJ – 153 kcal – 8 g protein – 29 g carbohydrate – 1g sugars – 1 g fat – 0 g saturates – 0 g fibre – 480 mg sodium

HEALTHY TIP Prawns are an excellent source of protein and a great way to get iron, zinc and vitamin E. They have virtually no saturated fat.

QUAIL EGG SALAD WITH PRAWNS

Tiny quail eggs and prawns are an attractive combination, especially when they are combined with shredded mango and a delicious salad dressing.

INGREDIENTS 125 g (4 oz) raw prawns, large or medium sized │ 24 quail eggs │ 1 small mango or cooking apple, skinned and finely shredded │ 2 garlic cloves, finely chopped │ 4 shallots, finely sliced │ mixed salad leaves │ 1 long red chilli, stemmed, deseeded and finely sliced, to garnish

SALAD DRESSING 1–2 small red and green chillies, finely chopped │ 4 tablespoons lime or lemon juice │ 1½ tablespoons light soy sauce

ONE Make the salad dressing. Combine all the ingredients in a small bowl. **TWO** Prepare the prawns *(see page 11)*. **THREE** Fill a wok or steamer pan with water. Position the bamboo steamer basket or steamer rack in the pan, cover and bring the water to boil over medium heat. Taking care not to burn your hand, gently place all the quail eggs into the steamer basket and steam for 6–8 minutes. Pour in cool water, shell the eggs, halve them lengthways with a sharp knife and put them in a bowl. **FOUR** Place the prawns on a plate that will fit inside the steamer basket, cover and steam for 2 minutes. Remove the prawns and add them to the quail eggs. **FIVE** Add the mango, garlic, shallots and salad dressing and toss well. **SIX** Line a serving plate with mixed salad leaves and spoon over the egg salad. Garnish with the finely chopped chilli and serve immediately.

Serves 4 with 3 other main dishes

NUTRIENT ANALYSIS PER SERVING 684 kJ – 163 kcal – 14 g protein – 8 g carbohydrate – 7 g sugars – 9 g fat – 2 g saturates – 2 g fibre – 190 mg sodium

HEALTHY TIP Mangoes are rich in vitamins, minerals and antioxidants, high in fibre and low in calories and sodium. They are a good source of vitamin A and also contain vitamins B and C as well as potassium, calcium and iron.

recipe illustrated on pages 100–101

SPICY SEAFOOD SALAD

Finely sliced ginger is a perfect combination with seafood. Ideal for people on a diet, this dish can be eaten on its own or as a side salad.

INGREDIENTS 500 g (1 lb) mixed seafood, such as prawns, squid and small scallops | 4 tablespoons lime or lemon juice | 1 tablespoon fish sauce | 2 lemon grass stalks (white part only), each 12 cm (5 inches) long, finely sliced | 3 shallots, finely sliced | 2.5 cm (1 inch) fresh root ginger, peeled and finely sliced | 3–4 small red or green chillies, finely chopped, or ½–1 teaspoon chilli powder (or to taste) | 2 tablespoons finely chopped mint leaves | mixed salad leaves | mint leaves, to garnish

ONE Prepare the mixed seafood *(see page 11)*, cutting the squid into rings, rather than scoring it. **TWO** In a saucepan or wok cook the mixed seafood with the lime or lemon juice and fish sauce over medium heat for 2–3 minutes or until the prawns open and turn pink and all the seafood is cooked. **THREE** Stir in the lemon grass, shallots, ginger, chillies and mint leaves and mix well together. **FOUR** Line a serving plate with mixed salad leaves and spoon over the seafood. Garnish with a few mint leaves and serve immediately.

Serves 4 with 3 other main dishes

NUTRIENT ANALYSIS PER SERVING 500 kJ – 119 kcal – 20 g protein – 5 g carbohydrate – 1 g sugars – 0 g fat – 0 g saturates – 0 g fibre – 600 mg sodium

recipe illustrated on pages 104–105

POMELO AND PRAWN SALAD

This is an ideal dish for a hot, sunny day. Pomelo is wonderfully refreshing and its flesh has a unique, crumbly texture that melts in the mouth. When mixed with other ingredients in a salad its slightly sour taste enhances the flavour of the dish. Pomelo salad can be made with cooked meats such as chicken or pork, or, as here, with prawns. After peeling the pomelo you should be left with about 750 g (1½ lb) of flesh. If you can't find pomelo, use grapefruit instead.

INGREDIENTS 1.25 kg (2½ lb) pomelo │ 250 g (8 oz) raw prawns │ 75 g (3 oz) shallots, finely sliced │ 1 tablespoon roughly torn coriander leaves │ ½ long chilli, finely chopped │ 1½ tablespoons fish sauce │ 1½ tablespoons shredded dried coconut │ coriander leaves, to garnish

ONE Peel the pomelo *(see page 14)* and crumble the segments into their component parts, without squashing them or releasing the juice. **TWO** Prepare the prawns *(see page 11)*. **THREE** Cook the prawns in boiling water for 2 minutes and drain them. Transfer them to a mixing bowl and leave to cool. **FOUR** Add the pomelo to the prawns and gently combine with the shallots, coriander leaves, chilli and fish sauce. Sprinkle with shredded coconut *(see page 14)*, garnish with a few coriander leaves and serve immediately. If the pomelo is not sour (taste it!), add 3–4 tablespoons of lemon juice to provide a slightly sour taste.

Serves 4 as a starter

NUTRIENT ANALYSIS PER SERVING 487 kJ – 116 kcal – 7 g protein – 16 g carbohydrate – 14 g sugars – 3g fat – 2 g saturates – 3 g fibre – 615 mg sodium

HEALTHY TIP A relative of the grapefruit, pomelo is rich in vitamin C and potassium.

recipe illustrated on pages 108–109

RICE FLAKE SALAD

Rice noodles are more often used in soups than in salads, but this dish is an exception: a spicy noodle salad.

INGREDIENTS 500 g (1 lb) skinless chicken breast fillet | 500 g (1 lb) raw prawns, large or medium sized | 500 g (1 lb) rice flake (kua chap) noodles | 8 shallots, finely sliced | 2–3 spring onions, finely chopped | mixed salad leaves | coriander leaves, to garnish

SALAD DRESSING 3–4 small red chillies, finely chopped | 150 ml (¼ pint) lime or lemon juice | 2 tablespoons fish sauce

ONE Make the salad dressing. Combine all the ingredients in a small bowl. **TWO** Prepare the prawns *(see page 11)*. **THREE** Cook the chicken in a large pan of boiling water for 6–7 minutes or until it is done. Transfer the chicken to a mixing bowl and leave it to cool. Tear the chicken into long, thin threads. **FOUR** Cook the prawns in the same water for 2 minutes, then lift them out and put them in with the chicken threads. **FIVE** Gently drop the noodles into the remaining water and cook for 2–3 minutes or until they are cooked and soft. Drain the noodles and turn them into a bowl of cold water. Drain again and add them to the chicken and prawns. **SIX** Add the shallots, spring onions and salad dressing and combine well. Line a serving plate with a few mixed salad leaves and spoon over the rice flake salad. Garnish with a few coriander leaves and serve immediately.

Serves 4 with 2 other main dishes

NUTRIENT ANALYSIS PER SERVING 2834 kJ – 676 kcal – 45 g protein – 108 g carbohydrate – 3 g sugars – 5 g fat – 2 g saturates – 1 g fibre – 1290 mg sodium

FISH AND S

SEAFOOD

FISH WITH THREE-FLAVOUR SAUCE

You can vary the sauce served with this dish, using lemon juice for a clear sauce with a sharp taste or tamarind pulp for a thicker, darker sauce with a smooth, sour taste.

INGREDIENTS 1 red snapper or sea bream, about 450 g (14½ oz) | 3 garlic cloves, roughly chopped | 3 shallots, roughly chopped | 5 long red chillies, deseeded and roughly chopped | 3 coriander roots, roughly chopped | 2 tablespoons sunflower oil | 2 tablespoons Vegetable Stock *(see page 18)* or water | 2 tablespoons lemon juice | 1½ tablespoons fish sauce | 2 tablespoons palm or coconut sugar | Thai sweet basil leaves, to garnish

ONE Prepare the fish *(see page 10)*. **TWO** Use a pestle and mortar or small blender to combine the garlic, shallots, chillies and coriander roots into a rough paste. **THREE** Rub the outside of the fish with ½ tablespoon oil and grill or barbecue it on medium heat for 15–20 minutes on each side or until the fish is cooked and lightly browned. (You can place the fish in a fish-shaped griddle that opens out on a hinge. The fish is sandwiched between and is easier to lift and turn on the barbecue.) Transfer the fish to a serving plate and keep it warm. **FOUR** Heat the remaining oil in a nonstick wok or frying pan and stir-fry the garlic and chilli paste over medium heat for 2 minutes or until it is fragrant. Add the stock, lemon juice, fish sauce and sugar and cook for another minute or until the sugar has dissolved. **FIVE** Pour the chilli sauce over the warm fish, garnish with a few Thai sweet basil leaves and serve immediately.

Serves 4 with 3 other main dishes

NUTRIENT ANALYSIS PER SERVING 933 kJ – 222 kcal – 21 g protein – 15 g carbohydrate – 11 g sugars – 9 g fat – 1 g saturates – 0 g fibre – 600 mg sodium

HEALTHY TIP Chillies may help reduce blood cholesterol levels. Some reports indicate that eating chillies can help ward off gastric ulcers. They cause the stomach lining to secrete a mucus that coats and protects it from damage by irritants such as alcohol.

GARLIC PRAWNS

Only Thais use coriander roots in cooking, and if you can obtain them you'll see why we do. This is one of the best ways of stir-frying prawns and creates a very sophisticated dish.

INGREDIENTS 500 g (1 lb) raw large or medium-sized prawns | 5 garlic cloves, roughly chopped | 15 coriander roots, roughly chopped | 10 black peppercorns | 1½ tablespoons sunflower oil | 2 tablespoons Vegetable or Seafood Stock *(see pages 18 and 19)* **or water** | 1 tablespoon oyster sauce | 1 tablespoon light soy sauce | coriander leaves, to garnish

ONE Prepare the prawns *(see page 11)*. **TWO** Use a pestle and mortar to pound the garlic and coriander roots into a rough paste. Add the peppercorns and continue to grind roughly. **THREE** Heat the oil in a nonstick wok or frying pan and stir-fry the garlic paste over medium heat for 1–2 minutes or until it is fragrant. **FOUR** Add the prawns, stock, oyster sauce and soy sauce, stir-fry for another 2–3 minutes or until the prawns open and turn pink. Garnish with a few coriander leaves and serve immediately.

Serves 4 with 3 other main dishes

NUTRIENT ANALYSIS PER SERVING 458 kJ – 110 kcal – 11 g protein – 2 g carbohydrate – 0 g sugars – 6 g fat – 1 g saturates – 0 g fibre – 1030 mg sodium

STEAMED MUSSELS WITH LEMON GRASS

You can steam clams in exactly the same way as described here or, if you prefer, you can mix mussels and clams together to make this popular dish. Serve with Chilli and Lime Sauce *(see page 31)*.

INGREDIENTS 1 kg (2 lb) mussels in their shells │ 1½ tablespoons sunflower oil │ 4 garlic cloves, finely chopped │ 3 lemon grass stalks, cut into 2.5 cm (1 inch) lengths │ 3.5 cm (1½ inches) galangal, peeled and cut into 7–8 slices │ 1½ tablespoons fish sauce │ 1½ tablespoons lemon juice │ 2 long red chillies, stemmed, deseeded and finely chopped │ Thai sweet basil leaves, roughly chopped

ONE Prepare the mussels *(see page 11)*. **TWO** Heat the oil in a nonstick wok or frying pan and stir-fry the garlic, lemon grass and galangal over medium heat for 2–3 minutes or until fragrant. **THREE** Add the mussels to the wok and stir-fry for a few minutes. Add the fish sauce and lemon juice, loosely cover with a lid and cook over medium heat for 10–15 minutes, shaking the pan frequently. **FOUR** Cook until the mussels are open, discarding any shells that have not opened. Add the chillies and a few chopped basil leaves and mix together lightly, before serving in a large bowl.

Serves 4 with 3 other main dishes

NUTRIENT ANALYSIS PER SERVING 490 kJ – 117 kcal – 14 g protein – 2 g carbohydrate – 0 g sugars – 6 g fat – 1 g saturates – 0 g fibre – 420 mg sodium

STIR-FRIED SCALLOPS WITH BABY PAK CHOI

INGREDIENTS 300 g (10 oz) scallops, including the corals | 1½ tablespoons sunflower oil | 3 garlic cloves, finely chopped | 300 g (10 oz) baby pak choi | 1 tablespoon oyster sauce

ONE Prepare the scallops *(see page 11)*. **TWO** Heat the oil in a nonstick wok or frying pan and stir-fry the garlic over medium heat until it is lightly browned. Add the scallops and stir-fry for 1–2 minutes. **THREE** Add the baby pak choi and the oyster sauce, stir-fry for another 2–3 minutes and serve immediately.

Serves 4 with 3 other main dishes

NUTRIENT ANALYSIS PER SERVING 722 kJ – 172 kcal – 22 g protein – 7 g carbohydrate – 0 g sugars – 7 g fat – 1 g saturates – 0 g fibre – 360 mg sodium

HEALTHY TIP Dark green, leafy vegetables such as pak choi provide good amounts of vitamin C, as well as vitamin B6, folate and niacin.

FISH WITH GINGER SAUCE

This grilled or barbecued dish is another way of enjoying the combination of fish and ginger. Eat it at a main meal, alongside a soup or any curry or stir-fried dish.

INGREDIENTS 400–450 g (14–16 oz) red snapper, grey mullet, plaice or lemon sole | about 3 g (less than ¼ oz) dried black fungus | 2 tablespoons sunflower oil | 3–4 garlic cloves, finely chopped | 1 small carrot, finely sliced | 50 g (2 oz) fresh root ginger, peeled and finely sliced | 2 tablespoons Vegetable Stock *(see page 18)* or Seafood Stock *(see page 19)* or water | 1 tablespoon oyster sauce | 1 tablespoon light soy sauce

TO SERVE 2 spring onions, finely sliced diagonally | coriander leaves

ONE Prepare the fish *(see page 10)*. Soak the dried black fungus in hot water for 2–3 minutes or until it is soft. Drain and roughly chop it. **TWO** Rub the outside of the fish with ½ tablespoon oil and grill or barbecue the fish on medium heat for 15–20 minutes on each side until it is cooked and lightly browned. (You can place the fish in a fish-shaped griddle that opens out on a hinge. The fish is sandwiched in between and is easier to lift and turn on the barbecue.) Transfer the fish to a serving plate and keep it warm. **THREE** Heat the remaining oil in a nonstick wok or frying pan and stir-fry the garlic over medium heat until it is lightly browned. **FOUR** Add the carrot, ginger, dried black fungus and the remaining ingredients, and stir-fry for another 3–4 minutes. Pour the stir-fried mixture over the warm fish, garnish with the spring onions and a few coriander leaves and serve immediately.

Serves 4 with 3 other main dishes

NUTRIENT ANALYSIS PER SERVING 670 kJ – 160 kcal – 20 g protein – 4 g carbohydrate – 1 g sugars – 7 g fat – 1 g saturates – 0 g fibre – 320 mg sodium

HEALTHY TIP Ginger is known to be one of the best herbs for digestion, and it also improves and stimulates the circulation of blood throughout the body. It relieves nausea and lowers LDL (bad) cholesterol.

SPRING-FLOWERING CHIVES WITH SQUID

More fibrous in texture than either spring onions or true chives, Chinese chives are available in 'leafy' and 'flowering' types. This dish uses the tender stems of the spring-flowering chives, obtainable from oriental stores.

INGREDIENTS 500 g (1 lb) squid | 1½ tablespoons sunflower oil | 4 garlic cloves, finely chopped | 2 tablespoons Vegetable Stock *(see page 18)* or Seafood Stock *(see page 19)* or water | 1 tablespoon light soy sauce | 1½ tablespoons oyster sauce | 375 g (12 oz) Chinese flowering chives, cut into 5 cm (2 inch) lengths (discard the hard ends of the stems) | ground white pepper

ONE Prepare the squid *(see page 11)*. **TWO** Heat the oil in a nonstick wok or frying pan and stir-fry the garlic over medium heat until it is lightly browned. Add the squid, stock, soy sauce, oyster sauce and chives and stir-fry for 2–3 minutes or until all are cooked. Season with ground white pepper.

Serves 4 with 2 other main dishes

NUTRIENT ANALYSIS PER SERVING 682 kJ – 163 kcal – 22 g protein – 4 g carbohydrate – 2 g sugars – 6 g fat – 1 g saturates – 0 g fibre – 535 mg sodium

HEALTHY TIP In Asia, Chinese chives have been traditionally used as a herbal medicine to aid recovery from fatigue. They are a good source of vitamins A and C.

recipe illustrated on pages 128–129

RED CURRY WITH FISH AND TOFU

INGREDIENTS 300 g (10 oz) white fish fillets, skinned and roughly chopped │ 3 garlic cloves, roughly chopped │ 3 coriander roots, finely chopped │ ¼ teaspoon ground white pepper │ 1½ tablespoons cornflour │ 1½ tablespoons sunflower oil │ 1 quantity Red Curry Paste *(see page 24)* or 25–50 g (1–2 oz) bought red curry paste │ 200 ml (7 fl oz) can coconut milk, shaken well │ 200 ml (7 fl oz) Vegetable Stock *(see page 18)* or Seafood Stock *(see page 19)* │ 2 tablespoons fish sauce │ 1½ tablespoons palm or coconut sugar │ 200 g (7 oz) firm tofu, cut into 2.5 cm (1 inch) cubes │ 5 kaffir lime leaves, torn in half

TO SERVE Thai sweet basil leaves │ 2 long red chillies, stemmed, deseeded and finely sliced

ONE Blend together the fish fillets, garlic, coriander, ground white pepper and cornflour in a food processor or blender to make a smooth paste. Spoon it into a bowl. **TWO** Heat the oil in a nonstick wok or frying pan and stir-fry the red curry paste over medium heat for 2 minutes or until it is fragrant. **THREE** Add the coconut milk and stock. With a spoon or your wet fingers shape the fish paste into small balls or discs, about 2 cm (I inch) across, and gently drop them into the hot but not boiling coconut milk. Continue until you have used up the fish. **FOUR** Add the fish sauce and sugar and cook for another 5 minutes, stirring occasionally. **FIVE** Add the tofu cubes and cook for 1–2 minutes, taking care not to let the tofu cubes lose their shape. Add the kaffir lime leaves. Spoon into a serving bowl, garnish with Thai sweet basil leaves and chillies and serve immediately.

Serves 4 with 2 other main dishes

NUTRIENT ANALYSIS PER SERVING 1299 kJ – 311 kcal – 21 g protein – 21 g carbohydrate – 11 g sugars – 16 g fat – 7 g saturates – 1 g fibre – 720 mg sodium

CLAMS WITH GINGER

One of my favourite dishes, seafood with the refreshing taste of ginger is a delightful combination. Be sure to provide a spare dish for the shells.

INGREDIENTS 1 kg (2 lb) clams in their shells | 2 tablespoons sunflower oil | 4–5 garlic cloves, finely chopped | 4 tablespoons Vegetable Stock *(see page 18)* or Seafood Stock *(see page 19)* or water | 50 g (2 oz) fresh root ginger, peeled and finely sliced | 1 tablespoon oyster sauce | 1 tablespoon light soy sauce | 2 spring onions, finely sliced | coriander leaves, to garnish

ONE Prepare the clams *(see page 11)*. **TWO** Heat the oil in a nonstick wok or frying pan and stir-fry the garlic over medium heat until it is lightly browned. **THREE** Add the clams to the wok and stir-fry over medium heat for 4–5 minutes. Add the stock or water, ginger, oyster sauce, soy sauce and spring onions and stir-fry for another 2–3 minutes or until all the clams have opened. Discard any shells that have not opened. Spoon on to a serving plate, garnish with a few coriander leaves and serve immediately.

Serves 4 with 3 other main dishes

NUTRIENT ANALYSIS PER SERVING 558 kJ – 133 kcal – 15 g protein – 3 g carbohydrate – 0 g sugars – 7 g fat – 1 g saturates – 0 g fibre – 380 mg sodium

HEALTHY TIP Very low in saturated fat, clams are high in omega-3 fatty acids, which are vital for the development and function of the brain as well as for lowering blood pressure.

BLACK SESAME SEEDS WITH PRAWNS AND WATER CHESTNUTS

INGREDIENTS 250 g (8 oz) prawns │ ½ tablespoon black sesame seeds │ 1½ tablespoons sunflower oil │ 2–3 garlic cloves, finely chopped │ 200 g (7 oz) water chestnuts, drained and thinly sliced │ 125 g (4 oz) mangetout, trimmed │ 2 tablespoons Vegetable Stock *(see page 18)* **or Seafood Stock** *(see page 19)* **or water** │ 1 tablespoon light soy sauce │ 1 tablespoon oyster sauce

ONE Prepare the prawns *(see page 11)*. **TWO** Dry-fry the black sesame seeds in a small pan for 1 2 minutes or until they are fragrant then set them aside. **THREE** Heat the oil in a nonstick wok or frying pan and stir-fry the garlic over medium heat until it is lightly browned. **FOUR** Add the prawns, water chestnuts and mangetout and stir-fry over a high heat for 1–2 minutes. Add the stock and the remaining ingredients and stir-fry for another 2–3 minutes or until the prawns open and turn pink. Stir in the fried sesame seeds and serve immediately.

Serves 4 with 2 other main dishes

NUTRIENT ANALYSIS PER SERVING 488 kJ – 117 kcal – 8 g protein – 9 g carbohydrate – 1 g sugars – 6 g fat 1 g saturates – 1 g fibre – 550 mg sodium

HEALTHY TIP A very good source of calcium, black sesame seeds also have high amounts of protein, phosphorus, iron and magnesium. They can ease constipation and promote regular bowel movements.

SEAFOOD WITH CHILLIES

If you want a colourful stir-fry, try my seafood with chillies. Serve with Boiled Jasmine Rice *(see page 36)*.

INGREDIENTS 450 g (14½ oz) mixed seafood, such as prawns, squid, small scallops and white fish fillets (cod or sea bass) │ 1½ tablespoons sunflower oil │ 3–4 garlic cloves, finely chopped │ 125 g (4 oz) red pepper, deseeded and cut into bite-sized pieces │ 1 small onion, cut into eighths │ 1 carrot, cut into matchsticks │ 2.5 cm (1 inch) fresh root ginger, peeled and finely sliced │ 2 tablespoons Seafood Stock *(see page 19)* or water │ 1 tablespoon oyster sauce │ ½ tablespoon light soy sauce │ 1 long red chilli, stemmed, deseeded and sliced diagonally │ 1–2 spring onions, finely sliced

ONE Prepare the mixed seafood *(see pages 10–11)*. **TWO** Heat the oil in a nonstick wok and stir-fry the garlic over medium heat until it is lightly browned. **THREE** Add the red pepper, onion and carrot and stir-fry for 2 minutes. **FOUR** Add all the seafood, ginger, stock, oyster sauce and soy sauce and stir-fry for 2–3 minutes or until the prawns turn pink and all the seafood is cooked. **FIVE** Add the chilli and spring onions and mix well. Serve immediately.

Serves 4 with 2 other main dishes

NUTRIENT ANALYSIS PER SERVING 697 kJ – 167 kcal – 22 g protein – 7 g carbohydrate – 4 g sugars – 6 g fat – 1 g saturates – 1 g fibre – 720 mg sodium

STEAMED FISH WITH CHILLI AND LIME JUICE

INGREDIENTS about 450 g (14½ oz) pomfret, plaice, turbot, snapper or sea bream │ 3 garlic cloves, halved │ 4 whole spring onions │ 1 long red chilli, deseeded and finely chopped │ 1½ tablespoons lime or lemon juice │ 1 tablespoon light soy sauce │ ground white pepper

ONE Prepare the fish *(see page 10)*. **TWO** Fill a wok or a steamer pan with water, place the bamboo steamer basket or steamer rack into it, cover and boil over a high heat. **THREE** Place the fish on a deep plate that will fit on the rack of a bamboo steamer basket but is slightly larger than the fish. **FOUR** Add the garlic and spring onions and sprinkle over the chilli, lime or lemon juice and soy sauce. **FIVE** Taking care not to burn your hand set the plate inside the steamer basket and simmer for 10 minutes. Season with ground white pepper and serve immediately.

Serves 4 with 3 other main dishes

NUTRIENT ANALYSIS PER SERVING 506 kJ – 120 kcal – 21 g protein – 2 g carbohydrate – 0 g sugars – 3 g fat – 1 g saturates – 0 g fibre – 78 mg sodium

HEALTHY TIP Garlic's positive cardiovascular effects come partly from its sulphur compounds but also from its vitamin C, vitamin B6, selenium and manganese content.

MEAT AND

POULTRY

CHICKEN WITH MIXED VEGETABLES

INGREDIENTS 325 g (11 oz) mixed vegetables, including baby sweetcorn, green beans, asparagus spears and carrot | 1½ tablespoons sunflower oil | 3–4 garlic cloves, finely chopped | 325 g (11 oz) skinless chicken breast fillet, cubed | 4 tablespoons Chicken Stock *(see page 17)*, **Vegetable Stock** *(see page 18)* **or water** | 2.5 cm (1 inch) fresh root ginger, peeled and finely sliced | 2 tablespoons oyster sauce | 2 spring onions, finely sliced | coriander leaves, to garnish

ONE Prepare the vegetables. Cut the sweetcorn and beans in half. Trim the mangetout. Cut off the tips of asparagus and slice each stalk into 5 cm (2 inch) lengths. Cut the carrot into matchsticks. **TWO** Blanch all the vegetables in boiling water for 30 seconds, transfer to a bowl of cold water to ensure a crispy texture, then drain. **THREE** Heat the oil in a nonstick wok and stir-fry the garlic until it is lightly browned. **FOUR** Add the chicken and stir-fry for 3–5 minutes or until the meat is cooked. **FIVE** Add the mixed vegetables, stock, ginger and oyster sauce and stir-fry for 2–3 minutes. Add the spring onions. Serve immediately.

Serves 4 with 2 other main dishes

NUTRIENT ANALYSIS PER SERVING 708 kJ – 169 kcal – 20 g protein – 6 g carbohydrate – 4 g sugars – 7 g fat – 1 g saturates – 2 g fibre – 480 mg sodium

CHICKEN WITH CASHEW NUTS

Thais and Westerners alike enjoy chicken with cashew nuts. Stir-frying brings out a lovely aroma from the dried chilli, making it one of our classics.

INGREDIENTS 1–2 dried, long red chillies, about 12 cm (5 inches) long │ 1½ tablespoons sunflower oil │ 3 garlic cloves, finely chopped │ 500 g (1 lb) skinless chicken breast fillets, thinly sliced │ 3 tablespoons Chicken Stock *(see page 17)*, **Vegetable Stock** *(see page 18)* or water │ ½ red pepper, deseeded and cut into bite-sized pieces │ 1 small carrot, cut into thin strips │ 1 small onion, quartered │ 1½ tablespoons oyster sauce │ 1 tablespoon light soy sauce │ 2 spring onions, finely sliced │ 75 g (3 oz) dry-fried cashew nuts │ ground white pepper

ONE Remove the stems from the chillies, use scissors to cut each one into 1 cm (½ inch) pieces and discard the seeds. **TWO** Heat ½ tablespoon oil in a nonstick wok or frying pan and stir-fry the chillies over medium heat for 1 minute. Remove them from the wok. **THREE** Add 1 tablespoon oil and stir-fry the garlic for another 1–2 minutes or until it is lightly browned. **FOUR** Add the chicken and stock and stir-fry over a high heat for 4–5 minutes or until the chicken is cooked. **FIVE** Add the red pepper, carrot, onion, oyster sauce and soy sauce and stir-fry for 1–2 minutes. Add the spring onions, chillies and cashew nuts. Spoon on to a serving plate, season with ground white pepper and serve immediately.

Serves 4 with 2 other main dishes

NUTRIENT ANALYSIS PER SERVING 1334 kJ – 319 kcal – 32 g protein – 8 g carbohydrate – 3 g sugars – 18 g fat – 4 g saturates – 1 g fibre – 330 mg sodium

HEALTHY TIP Cashew nuts have a high vitamin C content, and they also contain iron, zinc, magnesium, selenium and vitamin B1. They have antiseptic and cicatrising properties and are considered good for toothache and gums.

recipe illustrated on pages 148–149

PANAENG CHICKEN CURRY

INGREDIENTS 1½ tablespoons sunflower oil | 1 quantity of Dry Curry Paste *(see page 23)* or 25–50 g (1–2 oz) dry curry paste from a packet | 750 g (1½ lb) skinless chicken breast, thinly sliced | 150 ml (¼ pint) can coconut milk, shaken well; reserve 2 tablespoons for garnish | 50 ml (2 fl oz) Chicken Stock *(see page 17)* | 1 tablespoon fish sauce | 1 tablespoon palm or coconut sugar | 2 tablespoons Tamarind Purée *(see page 33)*

TO SERVE 5 kaffir lime leaves, finely sliced | 1 long red chilli, stemmed, deseeded and finely sliced

ONE Heat the oil in a nonstick wok or frying pan and stir-fry the dry curry paste over medium heat for 2 minutes or until it is fragrant. **TWO** Add the chicken and stir-fry for 5 minutes. **THREE** Add the coconut milk, stock, fish sauce, sugar and tamarind purée or lemon juice and reduce the heat to low. Simmer, uncovered, for about 5–7 minutes. This is meant to be a dry curry, but you can add a little more water during the cooking if it dries out too much. Transfer the curry to a serving bowl, spoon the reserved warm coconut milk over the top, garnish with sliced kaffir lime leaves and chilli and serve immediately.

Serves 4 with 2 other main dishes

NUTRIENT ANALYSIS PER SERVING 1590 kJ – 380 kcal – 44 g protein – 13 g carbohydrate – 9 g sugars – 17 g fat – 7 g saturates – 0 g fibre – 480 mg sodium

CHICKEN LIVER WITH BLACK PEPPERCORNS AND GARLIC

The garlic and coriander root impart an intense flavour, but there is also a lovely smooth texture from the chicken liver in this dish. You can use thinly sliced calves' liver as an alternative.

INGREDIENTS 500 g (1 lb) chicken livers │ 5 garlic cloves, roughly chopped │ 10 coriander roots, roughly chopped │ 10 black peppercorns │ 1½ tablespoons sunflower oil │ 2 tablespoons Chicken Stock *(see page 17)*, **Vegetable Stock** *(see page 18)* **or water** │ 1 tablespoon oyster sauce │ 1 tablespoon light soy sauce │ coriander leaves, to garnish

ONE Trim the chicken livers and slice them into bite-sized pieces. **TWO** Use a pestle and mortar or a blender to pound or blend the garlic and coriander roots into a smooth paste. Add the peppercorns and continue to grind roughly. **THREE** Heat the oil in a nonstick wok or frying pan and stir-fry the garlic paste over medium heat for 1–2 minutes or until it is fragrant. **FOUR** Add the liver, stock, oyster sauce and soy sauce. Stir-fry for another 2–3 minutes or until the liver is light brown outside but a little pink and tender inside. Garnish with a few coriander leaves and serve immediately.

Serves 4 with 3 other main dishes

NUTRIENT ANALYSIS PER SERVING 912 kJ – 218 kcal – 25 g protein – 3 g carbohydrate – 0 g sugars – 12 g fat – 3 g saturates – 0 g fibre – 320 mg sodium

HEALTHY TIP Chicken liver is rich in vitamin A, which is good for the eyesight, skin and the immune system. Other nutrients include trace elements, such as iron, selenium and copper, which helps the formation of blood cells and connective tissue.

RED CURRY CHICKEN WITH THAI BABY AUBERGINES

This is a popular hot Thai curry made with a paste of dried red chillies and many fresh herbs. Using coconut milk cooked with chicken or whatever meat you prefer you can create your own favourite red curry. Baby aubergines from Thailand vary in size. In this recipe use aubergines about 1 cm (½ inch) across or quarter larger ones.

INGREDIENTS 1½ tablespoons sunflower oil | 1 quantity of Red Curry Paste *(see page 24)* or 25–50 g (1–2 oz) bought red curry paste | 450 g (15 oz) chicken breasts, thinly sliced 200 ml (7 fl oz) can coconut milk, shaken well | 200 ml (7 fl oz) Chicken Stock *(see page 17)* 200 g (7 oz) Thai baby aubergines | 2 tablespoons fish sauce | 1½ tablespoons palm or coconut sugar | 5 kaffir lime leaves, torn in half

TO SERVE Thai sweet basil leaves

ONE Heat the oil in a nonstick wok or frying pan and stir-fry the red curry paste over medium heat for 2 minutes or until it is fragrant. **TWO** Add the chicken and stir-fry for 2–3 minutes. **THREE** Add the coconut milk, stock, Thai baby aubergines, fish sauce, sugar and kaffir lime leaves and cook for another 5–7 minutes. Spoon into a serving bowl, garnish with Thai sweet basil leaves and serve immediately.

Serve 4 with 2 other main dishes

NUTRIENT ANALYSIS PER SERVING 1373 kJ – 329 kcal – 28 g protein – 14 g carbohydrate – 9 g sugars – 17 g fat – 7 g saturates – 2 g fibre – 740 mg sodium

HEALTHY TIP Thai baby aubergines have few calories and virtually no fat, and their meaty texture makes them a satisfying accompaniment to a delicious curry.

recipe illustrated on pages 156–157

STUFFED OMELETTE

A dish that is eaten occasionally rather than often, stuffed omelette needs to be made neatly, with the sides folded over the meat like a parcel.

INGREDIENTS 1 tablespoon sunflower oil | 2 garlic cloves, finely chopped | 125 g (4 oz) minced chicken or prawns | 1 carrot, cut into small dice | 1 small onion, finely chopped | 50 g (2 oz) petits pois, thawed if frozen | 50 g (2 oz) sweetcorn kernels, thawed if frozen | ½ red pepper, deseeded and cut into small dice | 1 tablespoon fish sauce | 2 tablespoons tomato ketchup

OMELETTE 3 large eggs | 1 tablespoon water | ground white pepper | 2 tablespoons sunflower oil

TO SERVE 1 long red chilli, deseeded and shredded | coriander leaves

ONE Heat the oil in a nonstick wok or frying pan and stir-fry the garlic over medium heat until it is lightly browned. Add the chicken or prawns and stir-fry for 3–4 minutes or until the meat is cooked. **TWO** Add the carrot and all the remaining ingredients and stir-fry for another 3–4 minutes. Keep this mixture warm while you cook the omelette. **THREE** Beat the eggs with the water until slightly frothy, and season with ground white pepper. **FOUR** Heat 1 tablespoon of oil in a nonstick pan and pour in half of the egg mixture. Swirl it around the pan so that it forms a thin omelette. When it has turned brown underneath and is almost set, gently flip it over to cook the top. **FIVE** Spoon half the filling into the centre of the omelette and carefully fold it up so that the filling is completely enclosed and the omelette forms a neat square. Keep it warm while you make another omelette in the same way. Serve both omelettes on a serving plate, garnished with chilli and a few coriander leaves.

Serves 4 with 2 other main dishes

NUTRIENT ANALYSIS PER SERVING 447 kJ – 107 kcal – 9 g protein – 9 g carbohydrate – 5 g sugars – 4 g fat – 1 g saturates – 2 g fibre – 360 mg sodium

HEALTHY TIP Eggs contain useful amounts of protein, which is essential for good health and well-being, plus vitamins A, B2, B12 and E.

YELLOW CURRY CHICKEN WITH PINEAPPLE

Chicken and pineapple are a typically Thai combination, which goes well with yellow curry both in colour and flavour.

INGREDIENTS 1½ tablespoons sunflower oil | 1 quantity of Yellow Curry Paste *(see page 21)* | 300 g (10 oz) skinless chicken breast fillet, thinly sliced | 200 ml (7 fl oz) coconut milk, shaken well | 200 ml (7 fl oz) Chicken Stock *(see page 17)* | 300 g (10 oz) pineapple, cut into 2.5 cm (1 inch) cubes | 1½ tablespoons fish sauce | 1 long red chilli, stemmed, deseeded and finely sliced, to garnish

ONE Heat the oil in a nonstick wok or frying pan and stir-fry the yellow curry paste for 2 minutes or until it is fragrant. **TWO** Add the chicken and stir-fry for 4–5 minutes. **THREE** Add the coconut milk, stock, pineapple and fish sauce. Spoon into a serving bowl, garnish with chilli and serve immediately.

Serves 4 with 2 other main dishes

NUTRIENT ANALYSIS PER SERVING 1124 kJ – 269 kcal – 19 g protein – 12 g carbohydrate – 9 g sugars – 16 g fat – 7 g saturates – 1 g fibre – 350 mg sodium

HEALTHY TIP Pineapple is high in the enzyme bromelain and the antioxidant vitamin C. Bromelain not only reduces the swelling, tenderness and pain of bruising but also helps to relieve indigestion. Vitamin C helps to decrease the severity of colds and infections.

recipe illustrated on pages 162–163

SPICY MINCED DUCK

This tasty dish is served on a medley of fresh crispy vegetables, making it a good healthy choice. It can also be made with minced chicken or pork.

INGREDIENTS 300 g (10 oz) minced lean duck | 3 tablespoons lemon juice | 1 tablespoon fish sauce | 1 lemon grass stalk (white part only), 12 cm (5 inches) long, finely sliced | 4 shallots, finely sliced | 5 kaffir lime leaves, finely sliced | 5 spring onions, finely chopped | 1 tablespoon ground rice *(see page 12)* | 3–4 small red or green chillies, finely chopped or ½–1 teaspoon chilli powder

TO SERVE mixed salad leaves | mint leaves | a selection of fresh vegetables, such as long green beans, tomatoes and cabbage

ONE Cook the duck, lemon juice and fish sauce in a nonstick saucepan or wok over high heat. Use a spoon to crumble and break up the duck until the meat has separated and cooked through. Remove from the heat. **TWO** Add the lemon grass, shallots, kaffir lime leaves, spring onions, ground rice and chillies to the duck and mix together. **THREE** Line a serving plate with a few mixed salad leaves, spoon the duck over them, garnish with mint leaves and serve immediately with crispy vegetables.

Serves 4 with 3 other main dishes

NUTRIENT ANALYSIS PER SERVING 585 kJ – 139 kcal – 17 g protein – 8 g carbohydrate – 2 g sugars – 4 g fat – 1 g saturates – 1 g fibre – 300 mg sodium

RED CURRY WITH DUCK AND LYCHEES

A luxurious but healthy dish, this is a curry you can enjoy with lychees, pineapple or young coconut if you prefer.

INGREDIENTS 500 g (1 lb) boneless duck breasts │ 1 teaspoon sesame oil │ 2 teaspoons light soy sauce │ 1 cm (½ inch) fresh root ginger, peeled and finely chopped │ 2 garlic cloves, finely chopped │ ½ teaspoon ground allspice │ 1½ tablespoons sunflower oil │ 1 quantity of Red Curry Paste *(see page 24)* or 25–50 g (1–2 oz) bought red curry paste │ 200 ml (7 fl oz) can coconut milk, shaken well │ 200 ml (7 fl oz) Vegetable Stock *(see page 18)* │ 2 tablespoons fish sauce │ 1½ tablespoons palm or coconut sugar │ 250 g (8 oz) can lychees, drained (discard the syrup) │ 125 g (4 oz) cherry tomatoes │ 5 kaffir lime leaves, torn in half

TO SERVE Thai sweet basil leaves │ 1 long red chilli, stemmed, deseeded and finely sliced

ONE Remove the skin and fat from the duck breasts and slice the meat thinly. Mix the meat with the sesame oil, soy sauce, ginger, garlic and allspice and set aside to marinate for at least 30 minutes. **TWO** Heat the oil in a nonstick wok or frying pan and stir-fry the red curry paste over medium heat for 2 minutes or until it is fragrant. **THREE** Add the meat, coconut milk and stock and cook for 5–6 minutes or until the meat is cooked. Add the fish sauce, sugar, lychees and tomatoes and cook for another 1–2 minutes, taking care not to let the tomatoes lose their shape. Add the kaffir lime leaves. Spoon into a serving bowl, garnish with a few Thai sweet basil leaves and chilli slices and serve immediately.

Serves 4 with 2 other main dishes

NUTRIENT ANALYSIS PER SERVING 1600 kJ – 383 kcal – 24 g protein – 29 g carbohydrate – 22 g sugars – 19 g fat – 8 g saturates – 2 g fibre – 780 mg sodium

HEALTHY TIP Duck is an excellent source of zinc and a good source of iron, providing three times as much iron as chicken. It has a similar protein content to chicken and turkey.

recipe illustrated on pages 168–169

STEAMED PORK SPARE RIBS WITH CORIANDER ROOTS

Everyone in Thailand loves this dish. The ribs need to be chopped to short lengths to fit the steamer rack. Ask your butcher to prepare them for you.

INGREDIENTS 1 kg (2 lb) pork spare ribs, chopped into 3.5 cm (1½ inch) lengths │ 3 garlic cloves, finely chopped │ 25 g (1 oz) coriander roots, cleaned and finely chopped │ 1–2.5 cm (½–1 inch) fresh root ginger, peeled and finely chopped │ 1 tablespoon light soy sauce │ 1 tablespoon oyster sauce

ONE Combine all the ingredients in a large mixing bowl, using your fingers or a spoon to mix them. Cover with clingfilm and leave to marinate for at least 3 hours or overnight in the refrigerator if time allows. **TWO** Fill a wok or a steamer pan with water, place the bamboo steamer basket on a steamer rack, cover and boil over high heat. **THREE** Place the marinated pork spare ribs on a plate. **FOUR** Taking care not to burn your hand set the plate inside the steamer basket and simmer for 20 minutes or until all the spare ribs are cooked. Check and replenish the water every 10 minutes or so.

Serves 4 as a starter or main course

NUTRIENT ANALYSIS PER SERVING 1020 kJ – 246 kcal – 23 g protein – 2 g carbohydrate – 0 g sugars – 16 g fat – 6 g saturates – 0 g fibre – 330 mg sodium

PORK WITH GINGER

INGREDIENTS about 3 g (less than ¼ oz) dried black fungus │ 1½ tablespoons sunflower oil │ 3–4 garlic cloves, finely chopped │ 500 g (1 lb) pork fillet or chicken breast, thinly sliced │ 1 small onion, cut into 8 pieces │ 5 cm (2 inches) fresh root ginger, peeled and finely sliced │ 1½ tablespoons oyster sauce │ 4 tablespoons Vegetable Stock *(see page 18)* **or** water │ 2 spring onions, finely sliced

TO SERVE coriander leaves │ ground white pepper

ONE Soak the dried black fungus in hot water for 2–3 minutes or until it is soft, then drain. **TWO** Heat the oil in a nonstick wok or frying pan and stir-fry the garlic over medium heat until it is lightly browned. **THREE** Add the pork or chicken and stir-fry for 4–5 minutes or until the meat is cooked. **FOUR** Add the dried black fungus and all the other remaining ingredients and stir-fry for another 2–3 minutes. Spoon on to a serving plate, garnish with a few coriander leaves, season with ground white pepper and serve immediately.

Serves 4 with 2 other main dishes

NUTRIENT ANALYSIS PER SERVING 1000 kJ – 240 kcal – 27 g protein – 4 g carbohydrate – 1 g sugars – 13 g fat – 4 g saturates – 0 g fibre – 325 mg sodium

TURIA WITH PORK

Turia, or Chinese okra, is a long, cucumber-shaped vegetable with ridges running along its length. It is available in many oriental stores.

INGREDIENTS 300 g (10 oz) turia | 1½ tablespoons sunflower oil | 3 garlic cloves, finely chopped | 175 g (6 oz) pork fillet, thinly sliced | 1 tablespoon Vegetable Stock *(see page 18)* or water | 1½ tablespoons oyster sauce | ground white pepper

ONE Use a knife to remove the skin of the turia and cut the flesh diagonally into slices 2.5 cm (1 inch) wide and 5 cm (2 inches) long. **TWO** Heat the oil in a nonstick wok or frying pan and stir-fry the garlic over medium heat until it is lightly browned. **THREE** Add the pork and stir-fry for 2–3 minutes. **FOUR** Add the turia, stock, oyster sauce and stir-fry for another 2–3 minutes or until the pork and turia are cooked. Season with ground white pepper and serve immediately.

Serves 4 with 2 other main dishes

NUTRIENT ANALYSIS PER SERVING 552 kJ – 132 kcal – 12 g protein – 4 g carbohydrate – 2 g sugars – 8 g fat – 2 g saturates – 3 g fibre – 270 mg sodium

HEALTHY TIP Turia is low in calories. A 75 g (3 oz) serving contains just 20 calories but 20 per cent of the recommended daily allowance of vitamin C.

BAMBOO SHOOTS WITH MINCED PORK

This dish from the northeast of Thailand has a lovely aroma and is quite spicy from the red curry paste. You won't need a curry dish if you have this as a main course.

INGREDIENTS 1½ tablespoons sunflower oil │ ½ quantity of Red Curry Paste *(see page 24)* or 20 g (¾ oz) bought red curry paste │ 175 g (6 oz) minced pork │ 300 g (10 oz) can shredded bamboo shoots in water, drained │ 1 tablespoon fish sauce

ONE Heat the oil in a nonstick wok or frying pan and stir-fry the red curry paste over medium heat for 2 minutes or until it is fragrant. **TWO** Add the minced pork and stir-fry until the meat has separated and cooked through. **THREE** Add the bamboo shoots and fish sauce and stir-fry for another 2–3 minutes.

Serves 4 with 2 other main dishes

NUTRIENT ANALYSIS PER SERVING 639 kJ – 154 kcal – 13 g protein – 6 g carbohydrate – 2 g sugars – 8 g fat – 2 g saturates – 2 g fibre – 430 mg sodium

HEALTHY TIP Low in calories and fat, bamboo shoots are so high in fibre that a single serving can provide as much as one-tenth of the recommended daily amount. They are also a rich source of potassium, which helps maintain normal blood pressure and heart rate.

GREEN CURRY BEEF WITH BAMBOO SHOOTS

Green curry is the classic Thai curry. It is more pungent than the other curries and should never be extremely hot.

INGREDIENTS 1½ tablespoons sunflower oil | 1 quantity Green Curry Paste *(see page 22)* or 25–50 g (1–2 oz) bought green curry paste | 450 g (14½ oz) tender rump or fillet steak, thinly sliced | 200 ml (7 fl oz) can coconut milk, shaken well | 200 ml (7 fl oz) Beef Stock *(see page 16)* | 150 g (5 oz) can shredded bamboo shoots in water, drained | 2 tablespoons fish sauce | 1½ tablespoons palm or coconut sugar | 50 g (2 oz) lesser ginger, peeled and finely sliced *(see page 13)* | 5 kaffir lime leaves, torn in half

TO SERVE Thai sweet basil leaves | 1 long red chilli, stemmed, deseeded and finely sliced

ONE Heat the oil in a nonstick wok or frying pan and stir-fry the green curry paste over medium heat for 2 minutes or until it is fragrant. **TWO** Add the beef and stir-fry for 2–3 minutes. **THREE** Add the coconut milk, stock, bamboo shoots, fish sauce, sugar and lesser ginger and cook for another 5–7 minutes. Add the kaffir lime leaves. Turn into a serving bowl, garnish with Thai sweet basil leaves and the sliced chilli and serve immediately.

Serves 4 with 2 other main dishes

NUTRIENT ANALYSIS PER SERVING 1484 kJ – 356 kcal – 28 g protein – 14 g carbohydrate – 8 g sugars – 21 g fat – 9 g saturates – 1 g fibre – 700 mg sodium

recipe illustrated on pages 176–177

MASSAMAN BEEF CURRY

This popular curry is typical of southern Thai cooking. Sweet flavours of mixed spices predominate, even though the curry is moderately hot. It is one of the very few dishes in Thai cooking that includes potatoes and roasted peanuts. If preferred, use lamb instead of beef.

INGREDIENTS 2 pieces cinnamon stick | 10 cardamom seeds | 4 star anises | 5 cloves | 1½ tablespoons sunflower oil | 1 quantity of Massaman Curry Paste *(see page 20)* or 50 g (2 oz) bought massaman paste | 750 g (1½ lb) beef flank or rump steak, cut into 5 cm (2 inch) cubes | 200 ml (7 fl oz) coconut milk, shaken well | 400 ml (14 fl oz) Beef Stock *(see page 16)* | 2 onions, quartered | 2 tablespoons fish sauce | 2 tablespoons palm or coconut sugar | 3 tablespoons Tamarind Purée *(see page 33)* or lemon juice | 75 g (3 oz) roasted peanuts *(see page 26)* | 250 g (8 oz) potatoes, cut into 2.5 cm (1 inch) cubes | 1 long red chilli, stemmed, deseeded and finely sliced, to garnish

ONE Dry-fry the cinnamon stick, cardamom seeds, star anises and cloves in a frying pan or wok over a low heat. Stir all the ingredients around for 2–3 minutes or until they are fragrant. Remove from the pan. **TWO** Heat the oil in a nonstick wok or frying pan and stir-fry the massaman paste over medium heat for 2 minutes or until it is fragrant. **THREE** Add the beef and cook for 2–3 minutes. Add the coconut milk, stock, onions, fish sauce, sugar, tamarind purée or lemon juice, dry-fried spice and roasted peanuts. Gently simmer over medium heat for 20 minutes. **FOUR** Add the potatoes and continue to simmer, uncovered, over low heat for another 30 minutes. Turn into a serving bowl, garnish with sliced chilli and serve immediately.

Serves 4 with 2 other main dishes

NUTRIENT ANALYSIS PER SERVING 2595 kJ – 620 kcal – 48 g protein – 38 g carbohydrate – 19 g sugars – 31 g fat – 11 g saturates – 4 g fibre – 780 mg sodium

HEALTHY TIP Onions contain two compounds, allicin and sulphoraphane, which are believed to reduce the risk of cancer. Some studies suggest that these compounds may also help to reduce blood cholesterol levels and reduce the risk of blood clots forming, thus helping to prevent coronary heart disease.

recipe illustrated on pages 180–181

BEEF WITH PEPPERS

INGREDIENTS 1½ tablespoons vegetable oil │ 3 garlic cloves, finely chopped │ 275 g (9 oz) tender rump or fillet steak, thinly sliced │ 3 tablespoons Beef Stock (see page 16), Vegetable Stock (see page 18) or water │ 125 g (4 oz) red and green peppers, deseeded and cut into bite-sized pieces │ 1 onion, sliced │ 1 tablespoon oyster sauce │ 2 spring onions, finely sliced │ ground white pepper

ONE Heat the oil in a nonstick wok or frying pan and stir-fry the garlic over medium heat until it is lightly browned. **TWO** Add the beef and stir-fry for 3–4 minutes. Add the stock, red and green peppers, onion and oyster sauce and stir-fry for another 2–3 minutes. Add the spring onions and turn on to a serving plate. Season with ground white pepper and serve immediately.

Serves 4 with 2 other main dishes

NUTRIENT ANALYSIS PER SERVING 689 kJ – 165 kcal – 16 g protein – 6 g carbohydrate – 4 g sugars – 9 g fat – 2 g saturates – 1 g fibre – 240 mg sodium

HEALTHY TIP Green peppers provide vitamin C and beta-carotene, both of which are believed to have protective antioxidant functions against cancer, heart disease and stroke.

VEGETABLES

STIR-FRIED MIXED VEGETABLES

Firm stir-fried vegetables retain their nutritional value better than boiled vegetables. They complement all Thai meat and fish dishes and can even be a meal in themselves. Vegetarians should omit the oyster sauce and increase the amount of light soy sauce to 2 tablespoons.

INGREDIENTS 10 thin asparagus spears | 10 baby sweetcorn | 125 g (4 oz) green beans | 125 g (4 oz) red and yellow peppers | 125 g (4 oz) small courgettes | 125 g (4 oz) mangetout, trimmed | 1 small carrot or 4–5 baby carrots | 1 tablespoon sesame seeds | 125 g (4 oz) small broccoli florets | 125 g (4 oz) bean sprouts | 2.5 cm (1 inch) fresh root ginger, peeled and finely sliced | 1½ tablespoons sunflower oil | 2–3 garlic cloves, finely chopped | 4 tablespoons Vegetable Stock *(see page 18)* or water | 1 tablespoon light soy sauce | 2 tablespoons oyster sauce | coriander leaves, to garnish

ONE Prepare the vegetables. Cut off the tips of the asparagus and cut each stalk into 5 cm (2 inch) lengths. Cut the sweetcorn and green beans in half lengthways at an angle. Halve and deseed the peppers and cut the flesh into bite-sized pieces. Slice the courgettes thinly. Leave the mangetout whole, although if they are rather large cut them in half and trim. Peel and cut the carrot into matchsticks or scrape them if you are using the whole baby carrots. **TWO** Dry-fry the sesame seeds in a small pan for 1 2 minutes or until they are lightly brown and set aside. **THREE** Blanch the asparagus stalks, baby sweetcorn, broccoli florets, green beans, courgettes, mangetout and carrot in boiling water for 30 seconds. Transfer them to a bowl of cold water to ensure a crispy texture, drain and put them in a mixing bowl with the asparagus tips, peppers, bean sprouts and ginger. **FOUR** Heat the oil in a nonstick wok or frying pan and stir-fry the garlic over medium heat until it is lightly browned. Add the mixed vegetables and all the remaining ingredients and stir-fry over high heat for 2–3 minutes. Turn on to a serving plate, garnish with a few coriander leaves and toasted sesame seeds and serve immediately.

Serves 4 with 2 other main dishes

NUTRIENT ANALYSIS PER SERVING 790 kJ – 190 kcal – 10 g protein – 19 g carbohydrate – 7 g sugars – 9 g fat – 1 g saturates – 6 g fibre – 430 mg sodium

HEALTHY TIP Asparagus and broccoli are excellent sources of folate, necessary for the production and maintenance of new cells. Broccoli also contains the phytochemical sulforaphane, which helps reduce the risk of cancer.

recipe illustrated on pages 190–191

STIR-FRIED MIXED VEGETABLES WITH TOFU

Thailand exports many tonnes of baby sweetcorn to the West, so you can use some real Thai vegetables for this dish. Vegetarians should use 2½ tablespoons of light soy sauce and no oyster sauce.

INGREDIENTS 500 g (1 lb) mixed vegetables, such as baby sweetcorn, thin asparagus spears, carrots, mangetout and bean sprouts │ 625 g (1¼ lb) firm tofu │ 1½ tablespoons sunflower oil │ 3 garlic cloves, finely chopped │ 2.5 cm (1 inch) fresh root ginger, peeled and finely sliced │ 2 tablespoons Vegetable Stock *(see page 18)* or water │ 1 tablespoon light soy sauce │ 1½ tablespoons oyster sauce │ coriander leaves, to garnish

ONE Prepare the vegetables. Cut the sweetcorn in half lengthways. Cut off the tips of the asparagus and slice each stalk into 5 cm (2 inch) lengths. Cut the carrot into matchsticks. Trim the mangetout. **TWO** Blanch all the vegetables in boiling water for 30 seconds, transfer to a bowl of cold water to ensure a crispy texture and drain. **THREE** Drain the tofu and cut it into 2.5 cm (1 inch) cubes. **FOUR** Heat the oil in a nonstick wok or frying pan and stir-fry the garlic over medium heat until it is lightly browned. **FIVE** Add the mixed vegetables, tofu and all the remaining ingredients and gently stir-fry for 2–3 minutes, taking care not to let the tofu cubes lose their shape. Spoon into a serving bowl, garnish with a few coriander leaves and serve immediately.

Serves 4 with 2 other main dishes

NUTRIENT ANALYSIS PER SERVING 1217 kJ – 290 kcal – 23 g protein – 22 g carbohydrate – 5 g sugars – 13 g fat – 2 g saturates – 8 g fibre – 330 mg sodium

STIR-FRIED MUSHROOMS WITH GINGER

There are so many health benefits from eating mushrooms that I have included a delicious combination using fresh ginger. It's just a side dish, but everyone will enjoy it. Vegetarians can use light soy sauce instead of the oyster sauce.

INGREDIENTS about 3 g (less than ¼ oz) dried black fungus │ 1½ tablespoons sunflower oil │ 3 garlic cloves, finely chopped │ 500 g (1 lb) mixed mushrooms, such as oyster, shiitake and button │ 1 small onion, cut into 6 wedges │ 3 tablespoons Vegetable Stock *(see page 18)* or water │ 2 tablespoons oyster sauce │ 5 cm (2 inches) fresh root ginger, peeled and finely sliced │ 2 spring onions, slivered │ coriander leaves, to garnish

ONE Soak the dried black fungus in hot water for 2–3 minutes until it is soft, then drain. Remove and discard the hard stalks. **TWO** Heat the oil in a nonstick wok or frying pan and stir-fry the garlic over medium heat until it is lightly browned. **THREE** Cut any large mushrooms in half and remove the hard stalks. Add the mushrooms and the remaining ingredients to the wok and stir-fry over a high heat for 4–5 minutes. Spoon on to a serving plate, garnish with a few coriander leaves and serve immediately.

Serves 4 with 2 other main dishes

NUTRIENT ANALYSIS PER SERVING 356 kJ – 86 kcal – 3 g protein – 5 g carbohydrate – 1 g sugars – 6 g fat – 1 g saturates – 3 g fibre – 425 mg sodium

HEALTHY TIP Mushrooms provide protein, fibre, B vitamins and vitamin C, as well as calcium and other minerals. Medicinal mushrooms, like shiitake, have been shown to boost heart health, ward off viruses and combat allergies, among other benefits.

recipe illustrated on pages 196–197

JUNGLE CURRY WITH MIXED VEGETABLES

This is a very hot curry that, unusually, does not use coconut milk, but it can be made with any kind of meat or seafood. Vegetarians should omit the shrimp paste and fish sauce and use 2 tablespoons of light soy sauce.

INGREDIENTS 2 dried, long red chillies, each about 5 inches (12 cm) long | 1 lemon grass stalk (white part only), 12 cm (5 inches) long, finely sliced | 2.5 cm (1 inch) fresh galangal, peeled and finely sliced | 3 shallots, finely chopped | 2 garlic cloves, finely chopped | 1 tablespoon finely chopped lesser ginger *(see page 13)* | ½ teaspoon shrimp paste | 375 g (12 oz) mixed vegetables, such as baby sweetcorn, green beans, Thai baby aubergines, carrots, courgettes and mixed mushrooms (oyster, shiitake and button) | 600 ml (1 pint) **Vegetable Stock** *(see page 18)* | 1 tablespoon fish sauce | 2–3 kaffir lime leaves, torn, to garnish

ONE Remove the stems and slit the chillies lengthways with a sharp knife, discard all the seeds and roughly chop the flesh. Soak it in hot water for 2 minutes or until it is soft, then drain. **TWO** Use a pestle and mortar to grind and pound the chillies, lemon grass and galangal into a paste. **THREE** Add the shallots, garlic, lesser ginger and shrimp paste and continue to pound into a smooth paste. **FOUR** Prepare the vegetables. Cut the baby sweetcorn and green beans in half lengthways at an angle. Slice the carrots and courgettes diagonally. Cut the mushrooms in half if they are large and remove and discard any hard stalks. **FIVE** Put the stock, chilli paste and fish sauce in a large saucepan and bring it to the boil. Add all the mixed vegetables and cook for another 4–5 minutes. Garnish with the kaffir lime leaves and serve immediately.

Serves 4 with 2 main dishes

NUTRIENT ANALYSIS PER SERVING 140 kJ – 33 kcal – 2 g protein – 5 g carbohydrate – 2 g sugars – 1 g fat – 0 g saturates – 3 g fibre – 210 mg sodium

HEALTHY TIP Green beans are a good source of vitamin B folate, which is essential for a healthy pregnancy. Doctors say it is important to ensure a good intake of folate in the early stages of pregnancy to prevent spina bifida.

BITTER MELON OMELETTE

INGREDIENTS 175 g (6 oz) bitter melon │ ½ teaspoon salt │ 4 large eggs │ 1 tablespoon light soy sauce │ 1½ tablespoons sunflower oil │ 3 garlic cloves, finely chopped │ ground white pepper │ **Sesame Oil Sauce** *(see page 30)*, **to serve**

ONE Clean and cut the bitter melon into 2.5 cm (1 inch) rings, discarding all the seeds. Cut each ring in half and cut out the hard inner sleeve, which is about 2 mm (⅛ inch) thick. Finely slice the bitter melon pieces, put them in a bowl, sprinkle salt over and mix together. Leave for 30 minutes so that the salt draws out the bitter taste of the melon. Rinse the bitter melon in water to remove the salt and drain. **TWO** In a bowl beat the eggs with the soy sauce until slightly frothy. **THREE** Heat the oil in a nonstick wok or frying pan and stir-fry the garlic over medium heat until it is lightly browned. Add the bitter melon and stir-fry for 2–3 minutes. **FOUR** Pour the egg mixture over the bitter melon and cook for 1–2 minutes or until lightly browned, then flip the omelette over to brown the other side. Turn it on to a serving plate, season with ground white pepper and serve with Sesame Oil Sauce.

Serves 4

NUTRIENT ANALYSIS PER SERVING 530 kJ – 128 kcal – 8 g protein – 1 g carbohydrate – 1 g sugars – 10 g fat – 2 g saturates – 0 g fibre – 320 mg sodium

SWEET AND SOUR MIXED VEGETABLES

Few dishes are as healthy as mixed vegetables, especially when they are lightly stir-fried rather than boiled. Vegetarians should replace the fish sauce with 1 tablespoon of light soy sauce.

INGREDIENTS 500 g (1 lb) mixed vegetables, such as baby sweetcorn, green beans, carrots, courgettes, cucumber and red and yellow peppers | 1 onion | 2 tomatoes | 250 g (8 oz) can pineapple slices in light syrup | 2 tablespoons Vegetable Stock *(see page 18)* **or water** | ½ tablespoon cornflour | 1½ tablespoons tomato ketchup | ½ tablespoon fish sauce | 1½ tablespoons sunflower oil | 3 garlic cloves, finely chopped | boiled rice, to serve

ONE Prepare the vegetables. Cut the sweetcorn and green beans in half lengthways at an angle. Cut the carrot into matchsticks. Cut the unpeeled courgettes and cucumber in half lengthways and then into thick slices. Core and deseed the peppers and cut the flesh into bite-sized pieces. Cut the onion into 8 slices and the tomatoes into quarters. **TWO** Drain the pineapple and cut each slice into 4 pieces. Mix the syrup (about 6 tablespoons) with the stock, cornflour, ketchup and fish sauce in a small bowl to make a smooth paste. **THREE** Heat the oil in a nonstick wok or frying pan and stir-fry the garlic over medium heat until it is lightly browned. Add the sweetcorn, beans, carrots, red and yellow peppers and onion and stir-fry for 4–5 minutes. **FOUR** Add the pineapple pieces, tomato and pineapple syrup mixture and stir together for another minute. Spoon on to a serving dish and serve immediately with boiled rice.

Serves 4

NUTRIENT ANALYSIS PER SERVING 590 kJ – 140 kcal – 3 g protein – 23 g carbohydrate – 18 g sugars – 5 g fat – 1 g saturates – 3 g fibre – 345 mg sodium

HEALTHY TIP Red peppers are an excellent source of vitamin C and are rich in beta-carotene. Both of these nutrients are powerful antioxidants, which can help combat the damaging effects of free radicals and help protect against many diseases, including cancer and heart disease.

recipe illustrated on pages 204–205

VEGETABLE CURRY

There are so many curried meat dishes that it is easy to forget that vegetarians can enjoy curry, too. This one is really delicious. Vegetarians should use Vegetable Stock *(see page 18)* instead of chicken stock and light soy sauce instead of fish sauce.

INGREDIENTS 1½ tablespoons vegetable oil │ 1 quantity Dry Curry Paste *(see page 23)* or 25–50 g (1–2 oz) bought dry curry paste │ 150 ml (¼ pint) can coconut milk, shaken well │ 50 ml (2 fl oz) Chicken Stock *(see page 17)* or water │ 200 g (7 oz) sugarsnap peas, trimmed │ 125 g (4 oz) carrots, cut into matchsticks │ 125 g (4 oz) baby sweetcorn, cut in half lengthways │ 150 g (5 oz) pineapple, cut into bite-sized pieces │ 150 g (5 oz) cherry tomatoes │ 2 tablespoons Tamarind Purée *(see page 33)* or lemon juice │ 1 tablespoon fish sauce │ 1 tablespoon palm or coconut sugar │ 2 kaffir lime leaves │ 1 long red chilli, stemmed, deseeded and finely sliced, to garnish

ONE Heat the oil in a nonstick wok or frying pan and stir-fry the dry curry paste over medium heat for 2 minutes or until it is fragrant. **TWO** Add the coconut milk and stock and heat to boiling point. Add the sugarsnap peas, carrots and sweetcorn and cook for 3–4 minutes. **THREE** Add the pineapple, tomatoes, tamarind purée or lemon juice, fish sauce, sugar and kaffir lime leaves. Simmer, uncovered, for another 2–3 minutes. Spoon the curry into a serving bowl, garnish with the chilli and serve immediately.

Serves 4 with 3 other main dishes

NUTRIENT ANALYSIS PER SERVING 892 kJ – 218 kcal – 6 g protein – 22 g carbohydrate – 16 g sugars – 12 g fat – 5 g saturates – 2 g fibre – 720 mg sodium

HEALTHY TIP Sugarsnap peas provide good amounts of soluble fibre, which can help to lower high blood cholesterol levels. They are also a good source of vitamin C.

RICE AND N

OODLES

RICE SOUP WITH MINCED PORK

As an alternative to pork you can use chicken or prawns if you prefer. Spinach can be substituted for Chinese cabbage if this is proving to be difficult to find.

INGREDIENTS 3 coriander roots, roughly chopped │ 3 garlic cloves, roughly chopped │ ¼ teaspoon ground white pepper │ 400 g (13 oz) minced pork │ 1.8 litres (3 pints) Vegetable Stock *(see page 18)* │ 3 tablespoons light soy sauce │ 1 tablespoon preserved radish, finely chopped (optional) │ 625 g (1¼ lb) Boiled Jasmine Rice *(see page 36)* │ 2.5 cm (1 inch) fresh root ginger, peeled and finely sliced │ 50 g (2 oz) Chinese cabbage leaves, roughly chopped

TO SERVE 2 spring onions, finely chopped │ coriander leaves │ ground white pepper

ONE Use a pestle and mortar to pound the coriander roots, garlic and ground white paper into a paste. **TWO** Transfer the coriander paste to a bowl and combine it with the pork. **THREE** Put the stock in a saucepan and heat it to boiling point. Add the soy sauce, preserved radish (if used) and rice. **FOUR** Use a spoon or your wet fingers to shape the minced meat into small balls, about 1 cm (½ inch) across, and lower them into the rice soup. Cook over medium heat for 3 minutes. **FIVE** Add the ginger and Chinese cabbage. Cook for another 1–2 minutes. Spoon into a serving bowl, garnish with the spring onions and a few coriander leaves, season with ground white pepper and serve immediately.

Serves 4 as a main dish

NUTRIENT ANALYSIS PER SERVING 1487 kJ – 353 kcal – 25 g protein – 48 g carbohydrate – 0 g sugars – 8 g fat – 3 g saturates – 1 g fibre – 85 mg sodium

HEALTHY TIP Although pork today is leaner than ever before, it will be even healthier if you remove any visible fat. Pork contains high levels of vitamins B12, B6, thiamin, niacin and riboflavin and is also rich in phosphorus, zinc, potassium, iron and magnesium.

recipe illustrated on pages 214–215

RICE NOODLES WITH SEAFOOD

This noodle dish uses large white noodles and is one of the best known of its type. It is served at all times of the day or night in Thailand. Its light, bitter taste comes from Chinese kale.

INGREDIENTS 375 g (12 oz) dried white rice noodles, 1 cm (½ inch) wide │ 500 ml (17 fl oz) Seafood Stock *(see page 19)* │ 1 tablespoon oyster sauce │ 2 tablespoons light soy sauce │ 1 tablespoon black or yellow bean sauce (optional) *(see page 12)* │ 2 tablespoons cornflour │ 2½ tablespoons sunflower oil │ 5–6 garlic cloves, finely chopped │ 375 g (12 oz) Chinese kale, cut into 2.5 cm (1 inch) pieces, top leaves separated │ 500 g (1 lb) mixed seafood, such as raw, large or medium-sized prawns, white fish fillet (sea bass or cod), scallops and squid │ ground white pepper

ONE Soak the noodles in a bowl of water for 4–5 hours or, preferably, overnight. Drain them. **TWO** Mix the stock, oyster sauce, soy sauce, black or yellow bean sauce (if used) and cornflour in a bowl. **THREE** Heat 1 tablespoon oil in a nonstick wok or saucepan and stir-fry the noodles for 4–5 minutes or until they are cooked. Remove and keep them warm. **FOUR** Heat the remaining oil in the same wok and stir-fry the garlic over medium heat until it is lightly browned. Add the stalk of the Chinese kale and the mixed seafood and stir-fry for 2–3 minutes. **FIVE** Add the sauce mixture and top leaves of the kale and mix together for another minute or so. Spoon the mixed seafood and Chinese kale over the warm noodles, season with ground white pepper and serve immediately.

Serves 4 as a main dish

NUTRIENT ANALYSIS PER SERVING 2382 kJ – 569 kcal – 27 g protein – 90 g carbohydrate – 2 g sugars – 10 g fat – 1 g saturates – 3 g fibre – 790 mg sodium

HEALTHY TIP Chinese kale has abundant sulphur, and its juice is sometimes used for treating stomach and duodenal ulcers. It is an exceptional source of chlorophyll, calcium, iron and vitamin A.

THAI-FRIED NOODLES WITH PRAWNS

If you are cooking this dish in an average-sized wok or frying pan it will be easier to make it for two people at a time, using half the ingredients, and repeat. It is one of the most famous noodle dishes in Thailand.

INGREDIENTS 500 g (1 lb) large or medium-sized raw prawns, shelled and deveined │ 300 g (10 oz) dried sen lek noodles │ 4 tablespoons Tamarind Purée *(see page 33)* or lemon juice │ 2½ tablespoons fish sauce │ 3 tablespoons tomato ketchup │ 3 tablespoons sunflower oil │ 5 garlic cloves, finely chopped │ 4 eggs │ 2 carrots, shredded │ ½ teaspoon chilli powder (or to taste) │ 2 tablespoons ground dried shrimp │ 2 tablespoons preserved turnip, finely chopped (optional) │ 5–6 tablespoons chopped roasted peanuts *(see page 26)* │ 375 g (12 oz) bean sprouts │ 4 spring onions, finely sliced

TO SERVE 1 long red chilli, deseeded and shredded │ coriander leaves │ lemon wedges

ONE Prepare the prawns *(see page 11)*. Soak the noodles in water for 4–5 hours or overnight if time allows. Drain them. **TWO** Combine the tamarind purée or lemon juice, fish sauce and tomato ketchup in a bowl and set aside. **THREE** Heat 1½ tablespoons of oil in a nonstick wok or frying pan and stir-fry the garlic over medium heat until it is lightly browned. Add the prawns and cook for 1–2 minutes, then move the prawns from the middle of the wok. Add the remaining oil to the wok. Add the eggs and stir to scramble for 1–2 minutes. Add the noodles and carrots and stir-fry together for another 2 minutes. Add the tamarind purée or lemon juice mixture, chilli powder, dried shrimp, preserved turnip (if used) and half the roasted peanuts. Add half the bean sprouts and all the spring onions. Spoon on to a serving plate and sprinkle over the remaining peanuts. Garnish with chillies and coriander leaves, arrange the lemon wedges and remaining bean sprouts at the side of the dish and serve immediately.

Serves 4 as a main dish

NUTRIENT ANALYSIS PER SERVING 3111 kJ – 746 kcal – 45 g protein – 80 g carbohydrate – 8 g sugars – 26 g fat – 5 g saturates – 2 g fibre – 1260 mg sodium

recipe illustrated on pages 220–221

FRIED RICE WITH PRAWNS, CRAB AND CURRY POWDER

INGREDIENTS 250 g (8 oz) prawns, shelled and deveined | 3 tablespoons sunflower oil | 5–6 garlic cloves, finely chopped | 4 eggs | 1 kg (2 lb) cooked rice, stored in the refrigerator overnight | 250 g (8 oz) can crab meat, drained | 2 teaspoons curry powder | 1½ tablespoons light soy sauce | 1 onion, sliced | 2 spring onions, finely sliced | about 8 cooked crab claws, 125 g (4 oz) in total | ½ long red or green chilli, stemmed, deseeded and finely sliced, to garnish

ONE Prepare the prawns *(see page 11)*. **TWO** Heat the oil in a nonstick wok or frying pan and stir-fry the garlic over medium heat until it is lightly browned. Add the prawns and stir-fry over a high heat for 1–2 minutes. **THREE** Add the eggs and stir to scramble for 1–2 minutes. **FOUR** Add the rice, crab meat, curry powder, soy sauce and onion and cook, stirring, for 1–2 minutes. Add the spring onions. In the last minutes of cooking add the crab claws. Spoon on to a serving dish, garnish with the chilli and serve immediately.

Serves 4 as main dish

NUTRIENT ANALYSIS PER SERVING 2517 kJ – 598 kcal – 37 g protein – 79 g carbohydrate – 2 g sugars – 16 g fat – 3 g saturates – 6 g fibre – 570 mg sodium

FRIED RICE WITH PINEAPPLE

This is an easy way to enjoy fried rice with pineapple, which is a classic but sometimes complicated restaurant dish. You will find it easier to halve the ingredients and make sufficient for two people at a time, and then repeat the process.

INGREDIENTS 3 tablespoons sunflower oil │ 5 garlic cloves, finely chopped │ 300 g (10 oz) raw prawns │ 300 g (10 oz) ham, thinly sliced │ 50 g (2 oz) sweetcorn kernels, thawed if frozen │ 50 g (2 oz) petits pois, thawed if frozen │ 1 red pepper, deseeded and finely diced │ 2.5 cm (1 inch) fresh root ginger, peeled and finely sliced │ 1 kg (2 lb) Boiled Jasmine Rice *(see page 36)*, stored in the refrigerator overnight │ 2 tablespoons light soy sauce │ 300 g (10 oz) pineapple, cut into small cubes │ 50 g (2 oz) dry-fried cashew nuts

TO SERVE 1 large red chilli, seeded and finely shredded │ coriander leaves

ONE Heat the oil in a nonstick wok or frying pan and stir-fry the garlic over medium heat until it is lightly browned. **TWO** Add the prawns, ham, sweetcorn, petits pois, red pepper and ginger and stir-fry for 2 minutes or until the prawns open and turn pink. **THREE** Add the boiled rice, soy sauce and pineapple, mix together and cook over medium heat for 4–5 minutes. Spoon the fried rice on to a serving dish, garnish with the chilli and a few coriander leaves and serve immediately.

Serves 4 as a main dish

NUTRIENT ANALYSIS PER SERVING 2892 kJ – 688 kcal – 39 g protein – 90 g carbohydrate – 11 g sugars – 20 g fat – 4 g saturates – 6 g fibre – 940 mg sodium

HEALTHY TIP Pineapple is high in the enzyme bromelain and the antioxidant vitamin C. Bromelain is a natural anti-inflammatory agent that helps relieve the symptoms of rheumatoid arthritis while also breaking down the amino acid bonds in proteins, thus promoting good digestion.

FRESH EGG NOODLES WITH VEGETABLES

INGREDIENTS 2 tablespoons sunflower oil | 5–6 garlic cloves, finely chopped | 500 g (1 lb) egg noodles | 500 g (1 lb) mixed vegetables, such as mangetout, yellow or red peppers, small broccoli florets, baby sweetcorn, baby carrots, | 2 tablespoons Vegetable Stock *(see page 18)* **or water** | 1½ tablespoons oyster sauce | 1 tablespoon light soy sauce | 125 g (4 oz) bean sprouts | 3 spring onions, finely sliced | coriander leaves, to garnish

ONE Heat the oil in a nonstick wok or frying pan and stir-fry the garlic over medium heat until it is lightly browned. **TWO** Add the noodles and stir-fry over a high heat for 1–2 minutes. **THREE** Trim the mangetout. Deseed the pepper and cut the flesh into bite-sized pieces. Add the mixed vegetables, stock, oyster sauce and soy sauce and stir-fry for 3–4 minutes. Add the bean sprouts and spring onions and stir-fry for another minute or so. Spoon on to a serving dish, garnish with a few coriander leaves and serve immediately.

Serves 4 as a main dish

NUTRIENT ANALYSIS PER SERVING 2537 kJ – 600 kcal – 20 g protein – 99 g carbohydrate – 8 g sugars – 16 g fat – 4 g saturates – 8 g fibre – 835 mg sodium

FRIED RICE WITH SEAFOOD

Fried rice dishes always use rice that has been cooked, such as rice left over from a previous meal. A lovely mixture of seafood with fried rice makes a typical seaside dish, available all along the coasts of Thailand. If you are using a medium-sized wok, use half the ingredients at a time and repeat the process.

INGREDIENTS 500 g (1 lb) mixed seafood, such as raw prawns, scallops, squid and white fish fillet (cod or halibut) │ 3 tablespoons sunflower oil │ 4 garlic cloves, finely chopped │ 1 kg (2 lb) cooked rice, stored in the refrigerator overnight │ 2 onions, sliced │ 2.5 cm (1 inch) fresh root ginger, peeled and finely sliced │ 2½ tablespoons light soy sauce │ 3 spring onions, finely sliced │ 1 long red or green chilli, stemmed, deseeded and finely sliced, to garnish

ONE Prepare the mixed seafood *(see page 11)*. **TWO** Heat the oil in a nonstick wok or frying pan and stir-fry the garlic over medium heat until it is lightly browned. **THREE** Add the mixed seafood mixture and stir-fry over high heat for 1–2 minutes. Add the cooked rice, onions, ginger, soy sauce and stir-fry for 3–4 minutes. Add the spring onions. Spoon on to a serving plate, garnish with the chilli and serve immediately.

Serves 4 as main dish

NUTRIENT ANALYSIS PER SERVING 2235 kJ – 530 kcal – 30 g protein – 83 g carbohydrate – 5 g sugars – 10 g fat – 1 g saturates – 5 g fibre – 180 mg sodium

HEALTHY TIP All doctors recommend that we eat seafood regularly. It is a lean source of protein, with plenty of omega-3, which helps prevent heart disease, eczema, arthritis, inflammation, auto-immune disease, hypertension, cancer and even depression.

recipe illustrated on pages 230–231

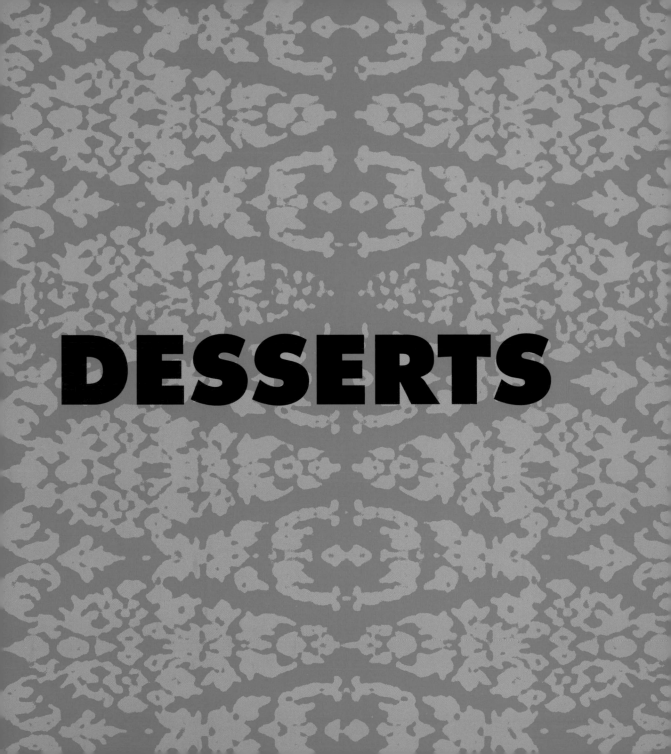

DESSERTS

WATERMELON SORBET

Thais know how to keep cool in hot weather, and there is no better way than eating this delightfully refreshing dessert.

INGREDIENTS 1.5 kg (3 lb) sweet red watermelon flesh, deseeded │ juice of 1 orange │ rind of half an orange │ 1 cm (½ inch) fresh root ginger, peeled and finely sliced

ONE Chop the watermelon into cubes and place in a food processor with the orange juice, orange rind and ginger. Process for 1–2 minutes or until smooth. **TWO** Pour the mixture into a freezer box and freeze for 1½ hours or until half-frozen. Take the mixture out of the freezer and whisk again in a food processor. Return to the container. Whisk at least twice more during the freezing time. There should be plenty of air whipped into the sorbet or it will be too icy and hard. Cover and freeze completely.

Serves 4–6

NUTRIENT ANALYSIS PER SERVING 540 kJ – 126 kcal – 2 g protein – 29 g carbohydrate – 1 g sugars – 1 g fat – 0 g saturates – 1 g fibre – trace sodium

HEALTHY TIP Watermelon is packed with some of the most important antioxidants in nature. It is an excellent source of vitamin C, a very good source of vitamin B6, and it also provides vitamin B1, magnesium and potassium.

QUAIL EGGS IN GINGER SYRUP

Quail eggs, a delicacy in Asia, make delicious starters and desserts. In this dish they are served with a delicious ginger syrup, an unusual but delightful combination.

INGREDIENTS 24 quail eggs │ 600 ml (1 pint) water │ 75 g (3 oz) soft brown sugar │ 2.5 cm (1 inch) fresh root ginger, peeled and thinly sliced

ONE Gently break the eggs one by one into a bowl and discard the shells. **TWO** Boil the water, sugar and ginger in a saucepan, until the sugar has dissolved. **THREE** Add the quail eggs and cook for 1–2 minutes until the yolks are half-cooked. Spoon the quail eggs and syrup into individual bowls, leaving the shredded ginger in the pan, and serve hot.

Serves 4 as a dessert

NUTRIENT ANALYSIS PER SERVING 800 kJ – 190 kcal – 10 g protein – 20 g carbohydrate – 20 g sugars – 8 g fat – 2 g saturates – 0 g fibre – 200 mg sodium

STICKY RICE WITH MANGO

This is one of the best known of all Thai desserts. In Thailand the mango season comes in April, when there are many varieties in the shops, some tasting better when they are green, crisp and crunchy, others when they are fully ripe.

INGREDIENTS 250 g (8 oz) white sticky rice *(see page 34)* | 100 ml (3½ fl oz) coconut milk | 50 ml (2 fl oz) water | 2 tablespoons palm or coconut sugar | ½ teaspoon salt (optional) | 4 ripe mangoes

ONE Soak the rice in a bowl of water for at least 3 hours. **TWO** Drain the rice and transfer it to a steamer basket lined with a double thickness of muslin. Spread the rice in the steamer. **THREE** Bring the water to a rolling boil. Taking care not to burn your hand set the steamer basket over the water, reduce the heat, cover and steam for 20–25 minutes or until the rice swells, and is glistening and tender. Check and replenish the water every 10 minutes or so. **FOUR** Mix the coconut milk, water and sugar in a small saucepan and stir over low heat until the sugar has dissolved. **FIVE** As soon as the rice is cooked, spoon it into a bowl, stir it into the coconut milk mixture, cover and leave to rest for 10 minutes. **SIX** Peel the mangoes and slice off the outside cheeks of each, removing as much flesh as you can in large pieces. Avoid cutting very close to the stone where the flesh is fibrous. Discard the stone. Slice each piece of mango into 4–5 pieces lengthways, arrange on a serving plate and spoon a portion of sticky rice with coconut milk beside them.

Serves 4 as a dessert

NUTRIENT ANALYSIS PER SERVING 1687 kJ – 400 kcal – 7 g protein – 80 g carbohydrate – 34 g sugars – 6 g fat – 3 g saturates – 4 g fibre – 35 mg sodium

HEALTHY TIP Mangoes contain an enzyme similar to papain in papayas, which acts as a digestive aid. They are high in fibre, low in calories and sodium, rich in vitamin A and are a good source of vitamins B and C as well as potassium, calcium and iron.

recipe illustrated on pages 242–243

SAGO PUDDING WITH WHITE LOTUS SEEDS

Sago palms (or, strictly speaking, cycads) grow profusely in Thailand, and their trunks provide a host for orchids. Sago pudding is a traditional Thai dessert, made from starch extracted from the pith of the sago palm. Lotus seeds are removed from the flowers and dried in the sun. They are widely available in Thai and oriental supermarkets, but if you cannot find them use fresh young coconut in this recipe instead.

INGREDIENTS 25 g (1 oz) white lotus seeds │ 150 ml (¼ pint) unsweetened coconut milk, well stirred, or milk │ 1½ teaspoons plain flour │ ¼ teaspoon salt │ 500 ml (17 fl oz) water │ 125 g (4 oz) sago or tapioca │ 50 g (2 oz) caster sugar │ coconut cream, to serve

ONE Soak the lotus seeds in boiling water for 30 minutes and drain. **TWO** In a small saucepan mix together the coconut milk or milk, flour and salt and cook over medium heat for 2–3 minutes or until slightly thickened. Transfer to a small bowl and set aside. **THREE** Boil the water with the lotus seeds briskly in a medium-sized saucepan. Add the sago and stir with a wooden spoon for a few minutes over medium heat. Keep stirring until the grains are swollen, clear and shiny. Reduce the heat if necessary. **FOUR** Add the sugar and stir until it has dissolved. The sago and lotus seeds should now be almost cooked. **FIVE** Leave the sago pudding to thicken for 10 minutes before spooning it into individual bowls with a few spoonfuls of coconut cream on top. Serve warm.

Serves 4 as a dessert

NUTRIENT ANALYSIS PER SERVING 1135 kJ – 270 kcal – 3 g protein – 47 g carbohydrate – 14 g sugars – 9 g fat – 4 g saturates – 0 g fibre – 165 mg sodium

HEALTHY TIP Lotus seeds are a mild sedative, helpful in calming the mind. They are rich in a repair enzyme that protects the plant from damage. Scientists have grown lotus plants from seeds that were over 1,000 years old.

BLACK STICKY RICE WITH EGG CUSTARD

Many different toppings are available in Thailand with this traditional dessert. Wrapped in a banana leaf it was once served at breakfast with tea or coffee but is now eaten at any time of the day.

INGREDIENTS 250 g (8 oz) black sticky rice │ 100 ml (3½ fl oz) coconut milk │ 50 ml (2 fl oz) water │ 2 tablespoons palm or coconut sugar

EGG CUSTARD 75 ml (3 fl oz) coconut milk │ 5 large eggs │ 250 g (8 oz) coconut or palm sugar, cut into small pieces if hard │ 1 teaspoon vanilla essence

ONE Soak the rice in a bowl of water overnight. **TWO** Fill a wok or steamer pan with water. Place in the bamboo steamer basket or steamer rack, cover and bring the water to boil over medium heat. **THREE** Meanwhile, make the egg custard. Mix together the coconut milk, egg, sugar and vanilla essence until the sugar has dissolved. **FOUR** Pour the custard through a sieve into a steamer bowl until it is three-quarters full. **FIVE** Taking care not to burn your hand, set the custard bowl inside the steamer basket, simmer for 10–15 minutes, until set around the edges and set aside. Leave to set at room temperature for about 30 minutes. **SIX** Drain and spread the rice into the same bamboo steamer basket over a double thickness of muslin. Cover and simmer for 30–35 minutes or until the rice swells and is glistening and tender. Check and replenish the water every 10 minutes or so. **SEVEN** Mix the coconut milk and sugar in a small saucepan and stir over low heat until the sugar has dissolved. **EIGHT** As soon as the rice is cooked, spoon it into a bowl. Stir in the coconut milk mixture, cover and set aside for 10 minutes. Serve the black sticky rice on a small dessert plate and spoon the egg custard over the top.

Serves 4 as a dessert

NUTRIENT ANALYSIS PER SERVING 2877 kJ – 684 kcal – 15 g protein – 123 g carbohydrate – 77 g sugars – 16 g fat – 7 g saturates – 1 g fibre – 150 mg sodium

HEALTHY TIP Although it's sometimes called glutinous rice, sticky rice is gluten-free. In black sticky rice a layer of bran covers the rice grains. Rice bran contains twice as much fibre as oat bran.

recipe illustrated on pages 248–249

FRESH FRUIT PLATTER

There is an abundance of fresh fruit in Thailand, especially pineapples, which are grown between rubber trees on huge plantations and are great to eat after seafood. Papaya is one of the most delicious of all tropical fruits, and watermelon is always refreshing on a hot summer day.

INGREDIENTS 1 fresh pineapple, ripe and yellow │ ¼ watermelon, sweet and red │ 1 small papaya, ripe and slightly orange │ ½ lime

ONE Use a large, sharp knife to chop off the crown and tail of the pineapple, then slice it vertically into four. Cut out the flesh, leaving enough of the outside shell to give a smooth underside, free of indentations. Discard the skin. Cut out the hard core from each quarter. **TWO** Put the pineapple on a large platter and cut it laterally into slices about 1 cm (½ inch) thick. Push the slices alternately 1 cm (½ inch) to the left and right to show that they are separate. **THREE** Slice the watermelon lengthways into two long pieces. Cut out the flesh and discard the skin. Put it next to the pineapple on the platter and slice it across in a similar way. **FOUR** Peel the papaya, discard the skin and slice it in quarters lengthways. Carefully scoop out the seeds from each quarter with a spoon, then use a sharp knife to pare away any remaining white seed lining. **FIVE** Place the quarters on the platter, make vertical cuts as before and arrange the pieces in a similar way. **SIX** Place the lime next to the papaya. Leave the fruit platter in the refrigerator for at least 20 minutes to cool. Squeeze the lime juice over the papaya when serving.

Serves 4–6

NUTRIENT ANALYSIS PER SERVING 724 kJ – 170 kcal – 2 g protein – 40 g carbohydrate – 27 g sugars – 1 g fat – 0 g saturates – 2 g fibre – 12 mg sodium

HEALTHY TIP Fresh fruit contain more healing properties than canned fruit. Pineapple is a good example, being rich in the enzyme bromelain (a natural anti-inflammatory agent), which is destroyed by the heat used in the canning process.

INDEX

ACKNOWLEDGEMENTS

I would like to thank everyone at Hamlyn who was involved with this project and helped to make it a success. I am grateful to my friends Rawipim Paijit ('Numwan'), Benjavan Kidhadamrongdet ('Ben'), and Chantra Robinson for their help and encouragement. My thanks are especially due to my partner John Lewell who has helped me with expressing my ideas and to our son Jonathan for his willingness to taste new dishes.

EXECUTIVE EDITOR Nicky Hill

EDITOR Charlotte Macey

DEPUTY CREATIVE DIRECTOR AND DESIGN Geoff Fennell

SENIOR PRODUCTION CONTROLLER Martin Croshaw

PHOTOGRAPHY William Reavell

FOOD STYLIST Tonia George

PROP STYLIST Liz Hippisley